BUILDING BRIDGES

Connecting Classroom and Community through Service-Learning in Social Studies

Edited by Rahima C. Wade

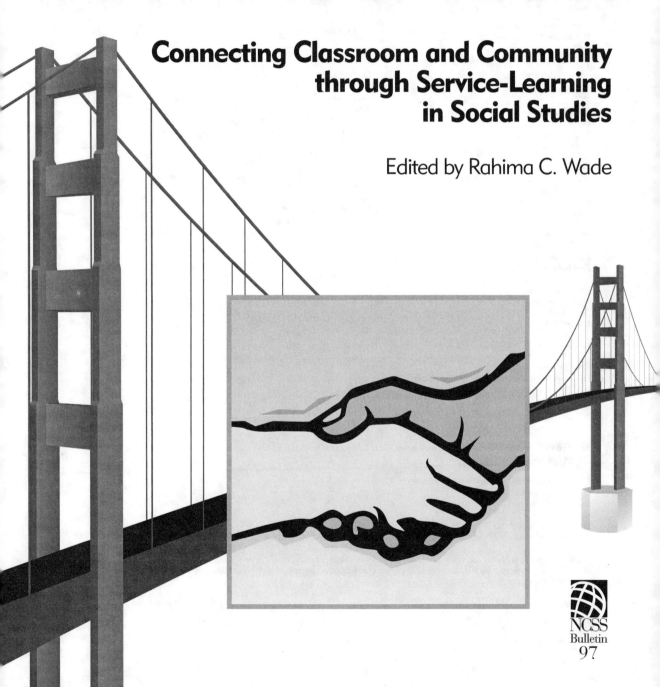

NCSS
Bulletin
97

National Council for the Social Studies
NCSS Founded 1921

Editorial staff on this publication: Michael Simpson, Terri Ackerman, David Morse
Design and Production: Gene Cowan

LIBRARY OF CONGRESS CATALOGING INFORMATION
ISBN 0-87986-083-9
PCN 00-105365

COPYRIGHT © 2000 BY NATIONAL COUNCIL FOR THE SOCIAL STUDIES
3501 NEWARK STREET NW • WASHINGTON DC 20016-3167 • WWW.SOCIALSTUDIES.ORG

PRINTED IN THE UNITED STATES OF AMERICA
10 9 8 7 6 5 4 3 2 1

TABLE OF CONTENTS

INTRODUCTION

Rahima C. Wade

As a social studies teacher with a commitment to the mission of my profession—developing an informed and active citizenry—I sometimes find it easy to become disheartened. I look at our society and see the growing divide between the have's and have-not's, too many children living in poverty, the institutionalization of racism limiting the health and well-being of the nation's people of color, and a citizenry who, by and large, care most about "what's in it for me" and little about trying to improve society through local civic efforts or state and national politics.

Despite these and other signs of the degeneration of our democracy, I have hope. The source of my hope is evident in the pages of this publication: the classroom teachers and their students who, with energy, determination, and creativity, are applying lessons learned in their social studies classrooms to active civic involvement in their communities. On a daily basis, the social studies teachers who share their stories here and many others like them across the country are taking the time to identify community needs and problems, to teach the necessary skills to make a difference, and to entrust their students to take action in the community on behalf of the common good.

The subject of this publication, which is the ninety-seventh bulletin of National Council for the Social Studies, is the method that these teachers are using to connect curriculum with community: service-learning. Service-learning is the most recent initiative in a long history of efforts both within and outside of schools to foster civic participation and volunteerism. The idea behind service-learning is to make the most of students' community service efforts, to connect them with academic skills and content, and to encourage students to reflect on and learn from their experience. Although service-learning projects can occur within any subject area, they have a particular suitability for the social studies, given the discipline's focus on the skills, values, and knowledge inherent in democratic participation.

In this bulletin, readers will find many examples of what service-learning can look like in the social studies curriculum. The projects described here go far beyond typical community service activities, such as volunteering an hour a week at a community agency. The teachers and students represented in these pages engage in civic participation through community partnerships, advocacy efforts, public policy making, and political action. They learn about complex social issues, how government works, and what to do when they face roadblocks in trying to create change. They also put valuable content and skills from their social studies curriculum to work in the process.

Although the term service-learning was coined sometime in the late 1970s, the movement to incorporate service in the academic curriculum has mushroomed in the last decade. As a social studies educator reading this bulletin, you have probably heard the term "service-learning" before. Perhaps you already incorporate service activities in your curriculum or are considering doing so. Unfortunately, most social studies classrooms are still based almost exclusively on the textbook, requiring students only to read, write answers to end-of-chapter questions, and periodically take tests covering the textbook material and class lectures. Whether you are an experienced service-learning practitioner or a teacher who is beginning to question the usefulness of the textbook-lecture-based curriculum in a democratic society, this bulletin has been written for you. It is my hope that the stories and information in this bulletin will provide you and other social studies teachers nationwide with new ideas and inspiration to get students of all ages directly involved in learning the lessons of citizenship firsthand.

Chapter 1 provides a definition of service-learning, an overview of the history of service and service-learning in our nation's history and in the social studies in particular, and a description of the necessary components for effective service-learning projects. Social studies teachers embarking on service-learning for the first time may want to use the list of components as a checklist for designing a quality project. Those experienced with service-learning will benefit from reflecting on their practice and seeking out new ideas to enhance their current civic education efforts.

Chapters 2 through 4 present twelve teachers' stories of their service-learning projects. From elementary through high school, the service-learning projects described in these pages illustrate the wide range of activities that can be labeled "service-learning." In an effort to assist readers to link these projects to their own curricula, each story begins by identifying the relevant NCSS standards for the project and listing the social studies curriculum objectives.

However, it is important to note that these projects are not meant to be replicated in other classrooms. As the stories here illustrate, effective service-learning projects grow out of course content, curriculum objectives, students' interests, and the needs of the local community. Thus, they cannot serve as blueprints for teachers embarking on service-learning. Instead they provide seeds for others' projects, new ideas to reflect on, and testimonies to the power of service-learning for enhancing students' commitment to being involved in their communities.

Readers will find an incredible diversity within these teachers' stories. Some projects take place within a single unit or course; others are multidisciplinary or involve the whole school. The projects described in these pages take place in urban, rural, and suburban settings from every region of the country. Collectively, they reveal that service-learning can be an effective component of any social studies classroom at any level.

Despite the differences in the stories, each project addresses important elements of quality service-learning experiences: careful planning, curriculum integration, structured reflection, student ownership, community input, and evaluation, among others. The teachers write honestly about their efforts, expose the challenges and shortcomings they faced, and exult in the positive outcomes they noted in their students and the communities they served. They describe the evolution of their efforts and note how factors outside of themselves, such as local regulations or students' experiences, affected the course of their projects. The teachers write about how they attempted to address the challenges they and their students faced in trying to understand complex social issues or create changes within societal bureaucracies, and how they enlisted personnel and financial support to assist them.

Most exciting, perhaps, are the outcomes for students and communities described in these stories. Projects grow and effect changes in ways the teachers themselves never could have envisioned. Students learn that community members will take them seriously and that youth have the power to make significant changes in their communities. Surveys reveal changes in students' attitudes and understanding of course content based on their service experience. Many students continue to be involved in civic activities as a result of their service-learning activities; some even choose a career based on their experiences in the community. These and other benefits of service-learning provide busy social studies teachers with increased motivation to continue their efforts to link students with their communities.

Teacher training in service-learning is essential if more students nationwide are to benefit from what service-learning has to offer. Chapter 5 focuses on service-learning in social studies teacher education, both at the preservice and in-service levels. Following a brief review of the literature on and several rationales for incorporating service-learning in teacher education, Joan Rose describes how she involves her social studies students in learning about service-learning as pedagogy.

Finally, Chapter 6 addresses challenges within public education, the social studies, and the service-learning movement that must be addressed if service-learning is to thrive in the new millennium. Although dedicated teachers will continue to involve their students in their communities despite the effort involved, more teachers will become involved with service-learning if schools, curriculum developers, and policymakers support them. The NCSS position statement issued in 2000, which is one of the Appendices in this bulletin, highlights the importance of such endeavors. The curriculum resources, journal articles, and national organizations listed in the other Appendix are already contributing to this effort. It is my sincere hope that you, one of the thousands of social studies educators across the nation who now has a copy of this bulletin, will also contribute to building bridges between the social studies classroom and the community through service-learning.

CHAPTER 1

COMMUNITY SERVICE-LEARNING IN THE SOCIAL STUDIES

Rahima C. Wade

Many social studies educators in our nation's classrooms are finding innovative ways to build bridges between the curriculum and the community through service-learning activities. Service-learning—the integration of community service with academic skills and content and structured reflection on the service experience—provides social studies students with opportunities to apply "book knowledge" to real problems and needs in the local community. Here are three examples of how students at different grade levels are fulfilling the mission of the social studies by becoming informed and active citizens.

- As part of a social studies unit on FDR and The New Deal, high school students compare New Deal legislation with present laws, develop recommendations for improving services to the needy, and work with a local social service agency to implement these changes.

- Elementary students interview senior citizens at a nearby nursing home to learn about schooling and childhood games in the past. They compare their interview results with both present-day children's games and those from the Colonial era and then develop a performance for the seniors on "The History of Children's Games."

- Middle school students studying immigration in their social studies class work after school at the local library helping to tutor recent immigrants to pass their U.S. Citizenship tests. They also write and distribute copies of "A Guide to Community Resources" to address new arrivals' needs for local transportation, health services, housing, and jobs.

These are just a few of the thousands of projects social studies educators have developed to enhance students' learning and address community concerns. These activities engage students in active citizenship while providing a meaningful context for learning social studies content and skills. Although the presence of service-learning activities in the social studies is growing, there are still too many classrooms in which students are relegated solely to reading and answering questions in textbook chapters. All social studies students deserve the opportunity to learn about the thrills and challenges of civic participation that service-learning provides. The purpose of this bulletin is to provide K-16 social studies educators with the information and practical ideas necessary to integrate service-learning in their curricula. This chapter focuses on providing a definition and history of service-learning, examining the research on K-12 student outcomes in service-learning programs, and outlining key components and useful strategies for effective service-learning projects.

DEFINING COMMUNITY SERVICE-LEARNING

Service-learning activities take a wide variety of forms, making defining the term a challenging task. In recognition of the need for a widely-accepted definition of service-learning, a group of service-learning educators formed the Alliance for Service-Learning in Education Reform (ASLER) and created the following definition:

> Service-learning is a method by which young people learn and develop through active participation in thoughtfully-organized service experiences that meet actual community needs, that are coordinated in collaboration with the school and community, that are integrated into each young person's academic curriculum, that provide structured time for a young person to think, talk, and write about what he/she did and saw during the actual service activity, that provide young people with opportunities to use newly acquired academic skills and knowledge in real life situations in their own communities, that enhance what is taught in the school by extending student learning beyond the classroom, and that help to foster the development of a sense of caring for others.[1]

Although most schools include some types of community service activities (e.g., canned food or clothing drives, fund-raisers, recycling programs), less often do teachers enhance students' learning from these experiences through integrating the service activity with academic skills and content and structured reflection on the service experience. Given social studies' mission of developing an informed and active citizenry, service-learning is a particularly important offering in the social studies classroom. Students not only develop civic participation skills, values, and attitudes; they also develop firsthand knowledge of the topics they are studying in the curriculum. Learning about the past from people who lived it, studying local history through artifacts and old buildings, learning about a culture through working alongside people from that culture, or developing an understanding of voting through coordinating a voter registration campaign provide social studies students with real-world understanding of social studies issues and an interest in social studies that can't be matched through textbook instruction alone.

A BRIEF HISTORY OF SERVICE AND SERVICE-LEARNING IN THE UNITED STATES

Service has a long-standing history in the United States, from the early history of Native peoples to the government programs of the 1990s. Although U.S. citizens are often seen as individualistic and competitive, our nation's history reveals a communal ethic that is evident in grassroots movements such as the abolition of slavery and the civil rights movement as well as children's organizations such as the Girl Scouts, Boy Scouts, and 4-H.

The history of service in government-sponsored programs can be traced back to the early 1900s. Some service programs promoted by presidents in office and deemed worthy enough for funding by Congress include the following: FDR's Civilian Conservation Corps, John F. Kennedy's Peace Corps, Lyndon Johnson's VISTA, and most recently, George Bush's Commission on National and Community Service and Bill Clinton's Corporation for National Service.

Notably in the 1980s, several privately sponsored initiatives also focused on developing youth service opportunities. Private corporations such as Ford, Mott, and Kellogg's have been instrumental in providing funding for the Campus Outreach Opportunity League in 1984, and Campus Compact, the National Association of Service and Conservation Corps, and Youth Service America, all in 1985.

Service moved into the school curriculum rapidly following federal funding during the Bush and Clinton administrations. Although the term service-learning is a relative newcomer on the educational scene (experiential educators trace it back to the early 1970s), the idea of service as an important part of the school curriculum was promoted much earlier by educational scholars such as John Dewey, Hilda Taba, and Ralph Tyler.[2] The service-learning movement in education has also been furthered by prominent national reports such as Carnegie's *Turning Points*,[3] support from national educational organizations such as the Association for Supervision and Curriculum Development and the National Association of Secondary School Principals, and calls for youth service in schools by prominent contemporary educators such as John Goodlad and Ernest Boyer.

THE LEGACY OF SERVICE IN THE SOCIAL STUDIES CURRICULUM

This history of service and civic action in the school curriculum can also be traced clearly in the development of the social studies. At the turn of the century, as our society shifted from rural to urban, educators realized the need for an explicit civic education in the schools. Although some educators advocated a social reconstructionist approach,[4] others, notably Arthur Dunn,[5] promoted service in the community as a central feature of the social studies curriculum.

Dunn, who later became a member of the 1916 Social Studies Committee, which greatly influenced the direction of social studies curriculum in the United States, taught community civics in Indianapolis schools as early as 1904. Dunn had his students identify specific community problems in the urban setting and then develop and apply their solutions. Perhaps the earliest description of something akin to service-learning was written by the civics subcommittee of the 1916 Social Studies Committee headed up by Dunn.[6]

> The good citizen can be defined as a person who habitually conducts himself
> with proper regard for the welfare of the communities of which he is a member, and who is active and intelligent in his cooperation with his fellow members to that end.[7]

What the committee then called "community civics" was to be offered throughout the grades, intensifying during "five periods a week" during the freshman year of high school. The specific aims of community civics included seeing the importance and significance of community welfare, knowing the social agencies that support these elements, and recognizing and responding to one's civic obligation through direct action in the community. The committee members highlighted that "He (the student) must be given an opportunity ... to *live* (italics in the original) his civics both in school and in the community outside."[8]

As the concept of service in the social studies curriculum moved from theory to practice, textbooks were developed for two courses of study, Community Civics and Problems of Democracy. The former course, however, lasted only a decade, and Problems of Democracy largely disappeared by the 1950s, both to be replaced by the more traditional lecture-worksheet approach and a heavy emphasis on historical and social science content knowledge.

The idea of service-learning in the social studies was again seriously considered in the 1960s through several programs and publications.[9] Service-learning was also promoted through National Council for the Social Studies (NCSS) publications and several methods textbooks.[10] Most recently, NCSS developed a Position Statement on Service-Learning (see Appendix 2 of this Bulletin) and a Special Interest Group on Civic Education and Service-Learning.

It is important to note that these efforts have not always coincided with widespread service-learning practice in the schools. The 1990s, however, find social studies educators across the nation increasing their use of service-learning, with support from these publications and federal and state funding for program development and teacher training.[11]

RESEARCH ON K-12 STUDENTS IN SERVICE-LEARNING PROGRAMS

The history of service in our society and the social studies provides a supportive backdrop for examining whether or not service-learning is a viable means of instruction in K-12 social studies classrooms. Ultimately, this question can best be answered by examining the research on K-12 student outcomes.

First, advocates of service-learning list numerous potential outcomes of students' involvement in serving the community. Educators have asserted that service-learning may positively influence the following aspects of student development: academic skills, problem-solving skills, critical thinking skills, ethical development, moral reasoning ability, social responsibility, self-esteem, assertiveness, empathy, psychological development, civic responsibility, political efficacy, tolerance and acceptance of diversity, specific skill acquisition relevant to the service tasks, and career goals and knowledge.[12] Some educators also claim that service-learning can lead to a decrease in behavior problems, increased enthusiasm for school, and students serving as positive role models for other students. Not all of these assertions are backed by the research; in fact, many of these issues have not thus far been thoroughly studied. A summary follows of the research on K-12 student outcomes in three areas relevant to social studies education: (1) academic development, (2) social and personal development, and (3) political efficacy and participation.

ACADEMIC DEVELOPMENT

Of key interest to many teachers is the question "Will service-learning involvement increase my students' learning of course content?" Unfortunately, the research addressing this question is neither extensive nor conclusive. In general, the few studies focusing on this question have revealed that the academic achievement of students performing service does not usually differ significantly from control students.[13] The good news in this finding is that service time spent outside the classroom does not reduce students' learning of course content. This assertion is supported by two studies in which active learning outside the classroom had no negative effects on academic achievement.[14]

There are, however, a few more promising findings in regard to academic development. Programs that involve cross-age or peer tutoring, in particular, seem to be effective in enhancing both tutors' and tutees' academic skills.[15] Shumer noted that service-learning students improved their attendance and school grades, as compared to a control group,[16] and Williams found that students engaged in fieldwork had higher grade point averages at the completion of their program.[17] Root noted in her review of the research on K-12 outcomes that when the service activity is carefully matched with course content, academic gains are greater (for example, internships in a local government office as part of a government course).[18] Also, several studies have shown that students engaged in service-learning develop greater higher level thinking skills than do control students.[19]

SOCIAL AND PERSONAL DEVELOPMENT

Conrad concluded that "the most consistent finding of studies of participatory programs is that these experiences do tend to increase self-esteem and promote personal development."[20] Overall, the literature suggests that personal and social development are the best documented outcomes of secondary school-sponsored community service programs.[21] Although not every study has been positive, numerous researchers have found gains in self-esteem, competence, or general self-worth as a result of participation in community service or service-learning programs.[22]

POLITICAL EFFICACY AND PARTICIPATION

Of great import to social studies educators is the question of whether or not service-learning leads to increased political efficacy and/or civic participation. Findings are mixed in this regard, yet it seems that service-learning experiences focusing specifically on local government or political issues are more likely than are other types of programs (such as volunteering in a day care center or building a nature trail) to lead to increased political efficacy.[23]

In regard to youth volunteer activities leading to future civic involvement, a series of studies conducted by The Independent Sector revealed that early community service experience is a strong predictor of volunteering for teens.[24] This finding is supported by several other studies as well. An early study of twenty-seven school-based programs suggested that service-learning is associated with reports of increased interest in volunteering in the future.[25] Also, a recent literature review revealed that high school students who participated in community service or school governance were more likely than were nonparticipants to be engaged in community organizations and in voting fifteen (or more) years later.[26]

Of considerable importance is the fact that schools play a critical role in whether youth get involved in their communities or not. Among teens who reported that their schools encouraged volunteer service, three quarters volunteered. "Regardless of race or ethnic background, if individuals are asked to volunteer they are more than three times as likely to volunteer than if they are not asked."[27] In a study by the Wirthlin Group, 74 percent of the teens surveyed indicated that they did not volunteer because they did not know how to get involved, while 60 percent said it was because they were never asked.[28] As in the Independent Sector studies, the Wirthlin Group found much higher involvement in community service when schools placed emphasis on its importance.

SUMMARY OF THE RESEARCH

What can social studies educators conclude from this brief review of the research on K-12 student outcomes? First, it is obvious that service-learning is not a "magic bullet" that will enhance every student's academic achievement, self-esteem, and future civic involvement. The research as a whole, however, points to the promise of thoughtfully structured experiences that bring about positive results. If social studies educators develop service-learning projects that involve teaching others what is being learned and/or carefully match the project activity to the curriculum, academic achievement is more likely. And at the very least, time spent outside of the classroom on service activities is unlikely to diminish students' academic learning. Additionally, almost all types of service-learning enhance students' personal and social development, and students appear to be much more likely to continue to be involved in their communities if they are encouraged to participate through the school curriculum.

These findings provide considerable support for service-learning among educators committed to the civic mission of the social studies curriculum. "Quality counts" and "context matters" are two critical edicts when considering the design of effective service-learning experiences. Most of the positive findings cited above came from studies that focused on exemplary service-learning programs (e.g., those that included substantial time spent on service and reflection and carefully matched learning and service goals). The next part of this chapter focuses on the essential elements of a quality service-learning project.

ESSENTIAL ELEMENTS OF QUALITY SERVICE-LEARNING

The definition of the Alliance for Service-Learning in Education Reform that was cited previously lists many of the essential elements of quality service-learning programs. Additional sources for more detailed discussion than can be provided here include the following: Principles of Combining Service and Learning;[29] Service-Learning: Core Elements;[30] and Community Service-Learning: A Guide to Including Service in the Public School Curriculum.[31] Seven central elements for quality service-learning programs are addressed here: preparation, collaboration, service, curriculum integration, reflection, celebration, and evaluation.

PREPARATION

Planning and preparing for a service-learning project are critical steps in fostering success. There are many ways to begin planning a project. Some social studies teachers start with their curricular goals and consider what types of service experiences will enhance course content and skills. Others, particularly at the elementary level, develop the service activity first and then create curriculum connections with social studies and other subject areas, such as language arts and math. With all projects, it is wise to begin by considering the parameters for the scope of the experience.[32] How much time do you want to devote to the service and reflection activities? Are there funds and transportation to support an out-of-school experience or would it be better to focus on a school-based need or problem? What community agencies are within walking distance of the school? Is there a particular issue that is of concern to you, your students, and/or the community? What types of service activities easily connect with your curricular goals?

Teachers should be sure to include all stakeholders in the planning of the project. Students and community agency members should have a say in how the project unfolds. Informing parents and administrators during the planning stage can help to address any concerns and potentially lead to additional resources and supporters. Are there other faculty or staff in the school that might work with you on this project?

Considering the logistical aspects of your service-learning project during the preparation stage may thwart potential problems down the road. Consider issues such as scheduling, transportation, and liability for off-campus activities. If your project will need funding, brainstorm possible avenues for acquiring this support. Will you need additional adults to help supervise students in the community? Oftentimes students can be especially helpful in coming up with ideas to address the logistical aspects of the project.

Orientation is another key activity during the planning phase. If students are going out into the community to work with others or help out at a community agency, they need to be prepared for this experience. Likewise, if the agency is new to student volunteers, it may be helpful to orient agency members in regard to their expectations of the students.

Finally, think about the learning component of your project during this early stage. How will you ensure that students connect their experience with the course content? In what ways and how often will you have students reflect on their experiences in the community? How will you evaluate student learning? Planning ahead will ensure that your project is a success, both in the community and in the classroom.

COLLABORATION

Service-learning projects generally involve several types of collaboration. First, it is likely that students will work together in small or large groups to carry out various aspects of the project. They may also be working directly with others in the community, perhaps serving senior citizens, preschoolers, or individuals with economic or health needs. Often the individuals with whom they are working are different from themselves culturally or in other significant ways. Do your students have the skills for these varied types of collaborations? If not, which civic education skills will be important to teach them in the classroom? Some possibilities include interview skills, conflict resolution strategies, or decision-making techniques. Minkler identified several democratic skills that students may use in conducting service-learning projects: respectful deliberation and dialogue, coalition building, developing creative solutions that meet everyone's needs, and gathering support from a broad audience in the community.[33]

As the teacher, it is likely that you will be collaborating with others with whom you have not been involved before. Think about who might be potential collaborators in your school, neighborhood, and local community. If you are approaching a particular community agency about a possible collaboration, be sure to consider the agency's point of view. Rather than propose a specific project, ask the agency director what needs or problems the agency is most concerned with at this time. Then brainstorm project possibilities with your students and agency members to develop a plan that is mutually beneficial for all involved.

It is important to note that collaborations with community members are likely to change over time. Initial enthusiasm can lessen if a project is not conducted with care. Agencies may be cautious about taking on student volunteers if they have not previously done so. In a successful service-learning project, community members will come to value the services your students provide and continue to invest the agency's time and resources toward your collaboration.

SERVICE

True service is more than an action; it is an attitude, a relationship, and a way of being in the world. There are numerous types of service projects suitable for the social studies curriculum. Although the following categories are somewhat arbitrary, service experiences can be labeled as direct, indirect, or advocacy activities.

Direct service involves working with others in the school or community or hands-on involvement with animals or the environment. Students may work with senior citizens, younger children, individuals who are learning English as a second language, people with disabilities or illnesses, or people living in poverty. Whenever possible, individuals from these groups should be included in the planning phase of the project to ensure that the activities will be mutually beneficial for all involved. The best service-learning projects ensure that all individuals involved are contributing their skills, talents, and interests toward making the community a better place for everyone. Students can sometimes develop condescending attitudes toward those they are helping and may need to be reminded that service-learning should be about solidarity, not charity.

Indirect service activities are fund-raisers or collection programs that generate money or resources that can be contributed to an organization working on a community problem. Although indirect service activities are generally easier to coordinate because they can be completed at school, teachers should consider the value of students working directly with others as well. Following are just a few of the ways students and teachers can fund-raise for a worthy cause: passing the hat at a meeting; canvassing door to door or by telephone; holding a dance; sponsoring a performance; sponsoring a concert; screening a movie;

sponsoring a walk-a-thon, work-a-thon, or road race; creating a newspaper signature ad; organizing a festival or carnival; selling T-shirts, bumper stickers, buttons, etc.; holding a raffle; having a bake sale; having a yard sale; or coordinating a car wash. Students can organize schoolwide collections of the following items: canned food, newspapers and other recyclables, animal shelter supplies (food, toys), clothing, books, infant items (e.g., disposable diapers, formula, baby food), or personal hygiene supplies (e.g., toothpaste, soap, shampoo). A third type of indirect service project is an adoption program where students pay for the preservation of rainforest acreage or endangered species.

Perhaps the most useful types of service-learning experiences for social studies educators concerned with developing students' civic participation skills are advocacy activities. The following activities give students opportunities to share what they have learned with others in the community, to work for community improvement through social and political channels, and to learn a variety of methods for public communication. Most of these activities are more suitable for secondary students, though several could be adapted for the elementary level. Advocacy activities include the following: creating public displays; offering public performances; writing editorials; making public service announcements; lobbying public officials; developing and distributing pamphlets, leaflets, or flyers; speaking at public meetings; phoning public officials; writing letters to public officials; writing a newsletter; developing a speaker's bureau; setting up a public hearing; boycotting products or businesses; organizing a demonstration or protest; writing a news release; participating in a call-in radio show; writing a grant; circulating a petition; proposing a bill for a new law; being a youth representative on a local board or city council; campaigning for an issue, ballot item, or candidate; planning a news conference; making and putting up posters; conducting a survey or public opinion poll and publicizing the results; setting up a telephone hot line; holding a contest; developing and distributing awards; developing a program for public access TV; or setting up a web page or listserv.

Although all of these activities provide valuable learning opportunities for young citizens, they take time to plan and carry out. Sometimes social studies teachers are concerned that the time spent on service will take away from covering course content. Although teachers of older students sometimes counter this problem by having them complete service activities during out of school time, there are several facts important to keep in mind here. First, students rarely remember information they don't use for very long. Would you rather your students memorize thirty facts for a test this week and forget almost all of them two weeks later or would you rather your students learn ten facts and retain the information because they use these ideas and experience how the ideas apply to civic life? Service experiences not only enhance the application of classroom knowledge, but also increase the motivation to learn social studies content, when students realize that they can use their book knowledge to make a difference in their school or community.

CURRICULUM INTEGRATION

Curriculum integration is what distinguishes a valuable service-learning project from a useful community service activity. Thus, it is essential that the project be connected with academic skills and content. Many resources are available to assist social studies educators in brainstorming the ways service can enhance the curriculum (see the Appendix on Service-Learning Resources for Social Studies Educators at the end of this bulletin).

At the elementary level, teachers often integrate service-learning into a variety of subject areas. For example, a fourth grade classroom studying cultures around the world might read books about different types of bread and their origins and then use their math skills to bake several types of bread for the local soup kitchen. Kindergarteners might brainstorm and try out ways they can help at school and at home. A second grade unit on neighborhood helpers or a third grade curriculum on communities presents numerous opportunities for service activities. Fifth graders studying U.S. history might identify several grassroots movements that have contributed to change in our country (e.g., civil rights, women's movement, animal rights) and then choose one to get involved with. All of these projects could easily incorporate students developing their reading and writing skills.

At the secondary level, when the social studies curriculum becomes more discipline oriented, matching the service activity with the curriculum becomes an even more important task. Following are a few ideas for secondary level service-learning projects, based on commonly taught high school social studies courses.

U.S. HISTORY

- Interview senior citizens or long-time community members about a topic studied in the course. Write up the interviews and give them to the interviewees as an affirmation of their contributions.

- Conduct library and firsthand research to write a history of the local community and how its development has been influenced by national historical events.

- Assist a local historical society in cataloging items, planning educational programs, or other needed activity.

- Plan an educational program for younger students on the true story behind a chosen historical event.

- Make books on tape of historical fiction works for blind children.

- Trace a selected social issue in the community through history (e.g., immigration, health care, racism, poverty) and develop an action plan for addressing some part of the problem.

GOVERNMENT

- Work with a local group (e.g., League of Women Voters, NAACP) to conduct a voter registration drive.

- Tutor individuals studying for their U.S. citizenship tests.

- Research, develop, and distribute a brochure in several languages used locally to alert teens to their civil and criminal rights and responsibilities (e.g., draft registration for high school males).

- Set up a babysitting or transportation service to help those in need get to the polls on voting day.

- Develop and distribute a petition for a change in a local community policy that concerns teens.

- Research laws affecting immigrants to your state from other countries. Write to public officials to advocate for specific policy changes to improve the lives of immigrants.

- Analyze school board meeting agendas and participate in meetings with agenda items of concern to students.

WORLD HISTORY

- Research the social issues or environmental problems concerning a selected country or area of the world. Develop an indirect service project to raise funds or collect needed items to send to the area.

- Develop a speaker's bureau connecting high school students from different countries with elementary classrooms studying their cultures.

- Review current children's books at the local library on a selected country or area of the world. Recommend that out-of-date books be removed and research new books to be purchased. Conduct a story hour with several of the new books for elementary age children.

- Research the demographics of your community in terms of representation of world cultures. Interview individuals from these cultures about their problems and needs living in the community and develop an action plan to address one of those needs.

ECONOMICS

- Research local market prices on certain items and services (e.g., staple foods, auto repairs, entertainment) and develop and distribute a brochure to low-income individuals. Include a cost-benefit analysis based on recommended daily requirements and cost of items.

- Research the national and global economic components of a social issue (e.g., hunger, illiteracy, homelessness) and develop an action plan for addressing some part of the problem.

- Fund-raise to purchase rainforest acreage. Research the needs of indigenous peoples in a rainforest region (e.g., Brazil) and organize a collection of needed items for schoolchildren there.

- Create a video library for the high school on different careers by making five-minute videos of individuals in the community. Be sure to include a wide range of occupations and provide information about training needs and costs and potential salary range for each career.

- Publish a newsletter on comparative cost analysis for commodities popular among students (e.g., CDs, computer games).

REFLECTION

Reflection is a means for reliving or recapturing our experience in order to make sense of it, to learn from it, and to develop new understandings and appreciation. Reflection takes place throughout a quality service-learning project, not just at the end of the experience. Critical to students' willingness to reflect honestly and deeply is a classroom climate based on mutual respect, caring, and openness to divergent ideas. At the beginning of a service-learning project, encourage students to reflect on their assumptions, stereotypes, fears, desires, and other preconceived notions. During the time period students are engaged in service, they should focus on processing their feelings and experiences and on developing approaches to address challenges they are facing. The end of the service-learning activity is the best time for students to draw conclusions about their experience, to connect what they have learned from their experience with course goals and content, and to apply their knowledge to thinking about future civic involvement.

There are numerous ways to have students reflect in a service-learning project. Often teachers will encourage students to keep a journal about their experiences; discussion is also a frequently used method. Students will gain more from the reflection process when teachers structure the reflection activity to focus on specific aspects of their experience. For example, in addition to keeping a journal or discussing what happened at the service site, what problems were encountered, or how students felt, social studies teachers can foster students' learning by asking questions such as "What civic participation skills did you use during this project?" or "How did your experiences working with others in the community support or challenge what we learned about in the textbook?" Following are several questions teachers can use to help students reflect on a societal issue central to their service-learning project and the notion of citizenship generally.

SOCIETAL ISSUES

- What new knowledge have you learned about this issue through your service experience?

- What human needs or problems are created by this issue?

- How are individuals and groups in the community (nation, world) attempting to address this issue?

- What historical events have been connected with this issue?

- What are the current political, economic, and social contexts influencing this issue?

- In your opinion, what are the best approaches to trying to create positive change concerning this issue?

CITIZENSHIP

- What is a good citizen?

- What type of citizen do you think you will be when you grow up?

- What are the ways that citizens help their communities?

- How does a democracy depend on civic participation?

- What would happen in our democracy if everyone participated in public life?

- What would happen in our democracy if only a few individuals participated in public life?

- Is community service an essential component of good citizenship in a democracy?

- Why or why not?

In addition to keeping a journal and having a discussion, there are many other useful means for fostering students' reflections on their service experiences. They include creative writing, writing persuasive letters, concept mapping, writing a guide for future program participants, creating artistic expressions (theater, music, dance, visual arts), developing a schoolwide or community display, and presenting at a public meeting or conference. Many of these activities can also be used as a means for evaluating students' learning.

CELEBRATION

Celebrating students' service-learning efforts is not just a way to have fun at the end of the project. Celebration also serves a variety of other goals: publicizing the project, saying "thank you" to those who helped, developing new support for the program, and honoring and renewing the commitment of those who will continue to be involved. Celebrations can range from small student-only popcorn parties to large public events open to the entire community. Students should be encouraged to help plan the event and to think about ways that they can share the results of their efforts (e.g., photo display, video, slide show, awards presentations). Of course, food is a must. Be sure to offer some healthy, vegetarian, and/or wheat free items for those individuals who may be on restricted diets. Celebrations that bring together most or all of a project's participants can help everyone see the impact that the program has had on the community.

EVALUATION

Evaluation in a service-learning program serves several purposes. First, it is important to assess what students have learned from the experience. Was the particular service activity that was chosen effective in enhancing the course content and goals? Are students aware of the civic participation skills they used or developed during the project? What are students' views about the community impact of their efforts? In general, did they believe their efforts were successful? Do they plan on continuing to volunteer or participate in civic life in other ways? Social studies teachers can answer these questions through a variety of methods including tests, essays, writing assignments, individual interviews, or analysis of students' journals.

A second purpose of evaluation is to make modifications in the program. Distributing a brief survey or conducting phone interviews with project participants in the school or community can assist in the process of improving the project. Although surveys are perhaps the easiest means for collecting responses to the same questions from many individuals, phone or personal interviews may net more in-depth information or ideas that weren't even inquired about.

Sometimes teachers will need to collect evaluation data to provide to funding sources (as with a state or federal grant) or to justify continuation of the project to administrators. Some of the information needed can be gleaned from the evaluation measures described above. Often the most impressive data for these audiences, however, involves numbers of participants, hours spent on service, funds spent, funds saved by the agency due to students' efforts, and so forth. If you know you will need to compile these data by the end of the project, develop a system in the beginning for doing so. Students can keep track of their efforts via timesheets, and agency members can be informed ahead of time about information that will be requested.

CONCLUSION

Service-learning is an especially suitable strategy for the social studies, given the profession's mission of creating active and informed citizens. Teachers' success in conducting quality service-learning projects will be enhanced if they collaborate with students, school personnel, and community members; match service activities to course goals and content; and provide frequent and varied opportunities for students to reflect on their experience. Through thoughtfully structured service-learning projects, social studies teachers can provide their students with opportunities to connect the curriculum with community concerns and to develop their civic participation skills and attitudes while working on problems of concern in the community.

Notes

1. Alliance for Service-Learning in Education Reform, *Standards of Quality for School-Based Service-Learning* (Chester, Vt.: Author, 1993), 1.

2. C. W. Kinsley, "Creating New Structures-Community Service Learning," *Community Education Journal* 18 (Fall 1990): 2-4.

3. Carnegie Council of Adolescent Development, *Turning Point: Preparing American Youth for the 21st Century* (Washington, D.C.: Author, 1989).

4. Paul Hanna, *Youth Serves the Community* (New York: Appleton, 1936).

5. Arthur William Dunn, *Community and the Citizen* (Indianapolis, Ind.: Echo Press, 1906); Arthur William Dunn, ed., *Social Studies in Secondary Education* (Washington, D.C.: Government Printing Office, 1916); Arthur William Dunn, *Community Civics and Rural Life* (Boston: Heath, 1922).

6. J. L. Barnard, R. W. Carrier, A. W. Dunn, and C. D. Kingsley, *The Teaching of Community-Civics* (Washington, D.C.: Government Printing Office, 1915).

7. Barnard et al., cited in David Warren Saxe, *Social Studies in Schools* (Albany: State University of New York Press, 1991), 181.

8. *Ibid.*, 193.

9. Donald W. Oliver and James P. Shaver, *Teaching Public Issues in the High School* (Boston: Houghton Mifflin, 1966); Fred M. Newmann, *Education for Citizen Action* (Berkeley, Calif.: McCutchan, 1975); Maurice Hunt and Lawrence Metcalf, *Teaching High School Social Studies* (New York: Harper and Row, 1955/1968).

10. Mary A. Hepburn, ed., *Democratic Education in Schools and Classrooms* (Washington, D.C.: National Council for the Social Studies, 1983); Walter Parker and John Jarolimek, *Citizenship and the Critical Role of the Social Studies* (Washington, D.C.: National Council for the Social Studies, 1984); Donald W. Robinson, ed., *Promising Practices in Civic Education* (Washington, D.C.: National Council for the Social Studies, 1967); Linda Rosenzwig, *Developmental Perspectives on the Social Studies* (Washington, D.C.: National Council for the Social Studies, 1982); Shirley H. Engle and Anna S. Ochoa, *Education for Democratic Citizenship; Decision Making in the Social Studies* (New York: Teachers College Press, 1988); Hunt and Metcalf, *Teaching High School Social Studies, 1955/1968*; Fred M. Newmann and Donald W. Oliver, *Clarifying Public Controversy: An Approach to Teaching Social Studies* (Boston: Little, Brown, 1970); David Warren Saxe, *Social Studies for Elementary Teachers* (Boston: Allyn and Bacon, 1994).

11. For a more detailed discussion of the historical roots of civic involvement in the social studies, see Rahima Wade and David Warren Saxe, "Community Service-Learning in the Social Studies: Historical Roots, Empirical Evidence, Critical Issues," *Theory and Research in Social Education* 24, no. 4 (Fall 1996): 331-359.

12. M. N. Alt and E. A. Medrich, *Student Outcomes from Participation in Community Service* (Report prepared for the U.S. Department of Education, Office of Research, by MPR Associates, Berkeley, Calif., 1994); Wade and Saxe, "Community Service-Learning in the Social Studies," 1996.

13. Alt and Medrich, *Student Outcomes,* 1994; Alan Melchior and L. Orr, *Overview: National Evaluation of Serve-America, Subtitle B-1* (Cambridge, Mass.: Abt Associates and Brandies University Center for Human Resources, 1995).

14. R. Urie, *Student Aides for Handicapped College Students: Final Report and Manual* (Laurinburg, NC: St. Andrews Presbyterian College, 1971); University of Pittsburgh, *Evaluation Report for Senior Semester Program 1974-75* (Morgantown, W.V.: Author, 1975).

15. P. A. Cohen, J. A. Kulik, and C.-L. C. Kulik, "Educational Outcomes of Tutoring: A Meta-Analysis of Findings," *American Educational Research Journal* 19 (1982): 237-248; D. Hedin, "Students as Teachers: A Tool for Improving School Climate," *Social Policy* 17, no. 3 (1987): 42-47.

16. R. Shumer, "Community-based Learning: Humanizing Education," *Journal of Adolescence* 17, no. 4 (August 1994): 357-368.

17. R. Williams, "The Impact of Field Education on Student Development: Research Findings," *Journal of Cooperative Education* 27 (1991): 29-45.

18. S. Root, "School-based Service: A Review of Research for Teacher Educators," in *Learning with the Community: Concepts and Models for Service-Learning in Teacher Education*, ed. J. A. Erickson and J. B. Anderson (Washington, D.C.: American Association of Higher Education, 1997), 42-72.

19. D. Conrad, "The Differential Impact of Experiential Learning Programs on Secondary School Students" (Ph.D. diss., University of Minnesota, 1980); D. Conrad and D. Hedin, *Executive Summary of the Final Report of the Experiential Education Evaluation Project* (Minneapolis: University of Minnesota, Center for Youth Development and Research, 1982).

20. D. Conrad, "School-Community Participation for Social Studies," in *Handbook of Research on Social Studies Teaching and Learning*, ed. James P. Shaver (New York: MacMillan, 1991), 543.

21. D. Conrad and D. Hedin, *High School Community Service: A Review of Research and Programs* (Washington, D.C.: Office of Educational Research and Improvement [ERIC Document Reproduction Service no. 313569], 1989); Dwight E. Giles, Jr., and J. Eyler, "The Impact of a College Community Service Laboratory on Students' Personal, Social, and Cognitive Outcomes," *Journal of Adolescence* 17 (August 1994): 327-340; Williams, "The Impact of Field Education," 1991.

22. T. W. Beister, K. Kershner, and M. W. Blair, "Evaluation of Cumulative Effects of RBS Career Education," (Paper presented at the annual meeting of the American Education Research Association, Toronto, Ontario, Canada, March 1978); Conrad and Hedin, *Executive Summary*, 1982; Conrad and Hedin, *High School Community Service*, 1989; S. F. Hamilton and L. M. Fenzel, "The Impact of Volunteer Experience on Adolescent Social Development: Evidence of Program Effects," *Journal of Adolescent Research* 3, no. 1 (1988): 65-80; Hedin, "Students as Teachers," 1987; Fred M. Newmann and R. A. Rutter, *The Effects of High School Community Service Programs on Students' Social Development* (Madison, Wis.: Wisconsin Center for Education Research, University of Wisconsin, 1983); W. G. Sager, "A Study of Changes in Attitudes, Values, and Self-concepts of Senior High Youth While Working as Full-time Volunteers with Institutionalized Mentally Retarded People" (Ph.D. diss., University of South Dakota, 1973); Norman A. Sprinthall and Ralph. L. Mosher, eds., *Value Development as the Aim of Education* (Schenectady, N.Y.: Character Research Press, 1978); University of Pittsburgh, *Evaluation Report*, 1975; Urie, *Student Aides for Handicapped College Students*, 1971.

23. Rahima Wade, ed., *Community Service-Learning: A Guide to Including Service in the Public School Curriculum* (Albany: State University of New York Press, 1997).

24. Virginia A. Hodgkinson and Murray S. Weitzman (with S. M. Noga and H. A. Gorski), *Giving and Volunteering in the United States* (Washington, D.C.: Independent Sector, 1992a); Virginia A. Hodgkinson and Murray S. Weitzman, *Giving and Volunteering Among American Teenagers 12 to 17 Years of Age* (Washington, D.C.: Independent Sector, 1992b).

25. Conrad and Hedin, *Executive Summary*, 1982.
26. J. Youniss, J. A. McLellan, and M. Yates, "What We Know About Engendering Civic Society," *American Behavioral Scientist* 40 (1997): 620-631.
27. Paul G. Schervish, Virginia A. Hodgkinson, Margaret Gates, and Associates, *Care and Community in Modern Society: Passing on the Tradition of Service to Future Generations* (Washington, D.C.: Independent Sector, 1995).
28. Wirthlin Group, *The Prudential Spirit of Youth Community Survey* (Newark, N.J.: The Prudential, 1995).
29. Dwight Giles, Elenn Porter Honnet, and Sally Migliore, *Research Agenda for Combining Service and Learning in the 1990s* (Raleigh, N.C.: National Society for Experiential Education, 1991).
30. M. Langseth, "Service-Learning: Core Elements," *The Generator* 10 (Spring 1990): 6.
31. Wade, *Community Service-Learning*, 1997.
32. Lillian S. Stephens, *The Complete Guide to Learning Through Community Service. Grades K-9* (Boston: Allyn and Bacon, 1995).
33. J. Minkler, "Service Learning," in *The American Promise Teaching Guide* (Los Angeles: Farmers Insurance Group, 1996), 151-185.

CHAPTER 2

SERVICE-LEARNING PROJECTS FOR ELEMENTARY SOCIAL STUDIES

The elementary years are an important time to lay the foundation for learning civic participation skills. Habits of mind and heart are set in the early years when students can learn that helping others is fun and can make a difference. This chapter tells the stories of four teachers who guided their young students to make a difference in their community and world. Kate Foley's first graders established a valuable cross-cultural partnership with Native American children at a Reservation School. Robyn Parks, a third grade teacher, took the risk of involving her third graders in learning about AIDS and in taking action on this controversial issue. In the B.I.G. Project, Helen Bergey facilitated 134 fourth graders learning about the past through conducting oral histories with senior citizens. Finally, Gerri Faivre shares the story of her school's involvement over a thirteen year period with marine environmental activism. All of these service-learning projects provide valuable connections to the elementary social studies curriculum, while giving young students the opportunity to learn about their community through firsthand involvement.

BOOK DRIVE FOR NAVAJO STUDENTS
Kate Foley
St. Paul's Episcopal Day School, Oakland, California

SUITABLE GRADE LEVEL(S):   1-3

RELEVANT NCSS STANDARDS:
- **❶ CULTURE**
- **❸ PEOPLE, PLACES, AND ENVIRONMENTS**
- **❹ INDIVIDUAL DEVELOPMENT AND IDENTITY**
- **❺ INDIVIDUALS, GROUPS, AND INSTITUTIONS**
- **❿ CIVIC IDEALS AND PRACTICES**

SOCIAL STUDIES OBJECTIVES:
1. Learn about different types of communities.
2. Understand how and why Native Americans were relocated to reservations.
3. Learn about the Navajo culture.
4. Learn about the present day lives of a Navajo community.
5. Discover similarities and common interests among children everywhere.

PROJECT DESCRIPTION:
Organizing a book drive for students at a school on the Navajo Nation created many opportunities for social studies lessons in my first grade classroom.

Before the school year started, I read an article in a teaching magazine about students having pen pals in classes on various Indian reservations across the country. I asked a class parent to call the Bureau of Indian Affairs in Washington, D.C., to see if they had a school for my class. The elementary education office of the B.I.A. matched my class with a first grade class at Rough Rock Community School in Chinle, Arizona. Serving the Navajo Nation, Rough Rock is a K-12 school offering programs for toddlers, adults, families, high school drop-outs, and out-of-town students.

In my classroom, the social studies unit on Navajo culture began before I introduced the idea of pen pals or possible service-learning projects. We discussed the settlement of the southwestern part of the United States and why the government moved so many Native American tribes to live only in designated areas. Although this is a difficult topic to explain to first graders, with the use of many visual aids and maps, I illustrated how people living in this country were relocated onto reservations. We talked briefly about the history of the Navajo people, including why and when they were forced to live on the reservation. Again using maps and posters, I included in this discussion the location of several other Indian reservations to illustrate to the children that the Navajo reservation was not the only reservation, nor is the Navajo Nation the only Native American tribe in our country. Next, the children found Chinle, Arizona, on individual maps, and outlined the boundaries of the Navajo reservation on a wall map of the state. The Chamber of

Commerce in Chinle had sent me several maps of the area, and other useful pictures, which I displayed in my classroom in our Social Studies Area.

During the early stages of the project, letter writing skills were introduced and taught while my first graders wrote letters to the first grade students at Rough Rock Community School on the Navajo Nation. When the first batch of letters arrived from Rough Rock, my students were eager and bursting with excitement. Our pen pals wrote about the community where they live, their school, their pets, and their favorite activities. They mentioned and illustrated horses and cattle running in their backyards, cultural celebrations in the community of Chinle, and favorite toys, and they asked what it was like to see the ocean. My class wrote back immediately, including stories about what it was like to go to the beach coupled with crayoned pictures of seashells and sand. Parts of their letters focused on what it was like to live in a city, the homeless people they see in the nearby park everyday, having a playground on the roof of our school, and how much they'd like to actually see a horse someday. They painted pictures of the ocean to send and enclosed school photos.

Among our objectives in first grade is a study of communities that takes place in the fall. The children had studied several communities before this project began so they were able to apply what they had learned earlier in the year to this project in several ways. Their questions to the students in Chinle often focused on aspects of "community" (e.g., Do you have a post office? Do you go to the movies? Is there a swimming pool?). The letters they received prompted further discussions about the many different kinds of communities that do exist in our country, and that living on an Indian reservation is only one example of many.

The letters from the Navajo children provided information that my students wanted to research further, which led to additional activities. Many discussions focused on the differences and similarities between our school and Rough Rock elementary. Our pen pals wrote about their classroom, their lessons, and their teacher, and we responded with descriptions and hand-drawn pictures of our inner-city school. These talks allowed me to bring into the discussion the other cultures we had studied during the school year to compare and contrast with what we were learning about the Navajo culture. We read stories in literature groups and as a whole class from the Navajo tradition.

In art class, the children studied Navajo blanket patterns and structures. Using a huge wooden loom, the children were able to weave their own small blankets as well as study how the blankets are made according to traditional methods. We dyed yarn with natural dyes and graphed blanket patterns on graph paper. A parent brought in a traditional Navajo blanket he had received from his grandmother. The blanket was unrolled in the middle of the classroom, while the children discussed the colors and patterns they had—until then—seen only in books. The children made hogans out of clay and paper mache. We talked about the hole left in the roof for smoke to pass through, and which direction the door traditionally faces when each dwelling is built. Our pen pals sent pictures, and the teacher I was writing to at Rough Rock sent photographs of her home. It was important for the first graders to see that many people on the Navajo reservation today still live in hogans, though not all.

Highlighted in the original article that I read was the fact that many of these schools were without basic supplies. I found out by writing to the first grade teacher that Rough Rock School desperately needed books. The school had a room designated as the library, but had no books. When we learned that the students at Rough Rock needed reading material, we discussed what that might be like—to go to a school where there is no library or weekly check out times. The children were interested in why the school had no books, while we have so many at our school, and wanted to know what we could do about it.

To begin the service aspect of our project, we discussed the important role that books play in our classroom. I asked the children to tell me their favorite stories, and I wrote the titles in a list on butcher paper. In math, we estimated how many books were on our shelves and talked about what it would be like not to have so many books. What would our classroom look like? Where would we go when it was our turn to visit the school library? What would we do with our third grade reading buddies? These are just a few of the many questions my first graders asked, as I continued to focus the many discussions on what it would be like to be without books.

I proposed that we try to find some books to send to Rough Rock, and the children immediately volunteered to look at home for old books they no longer used. I sent a letter home to the parents of my students outlining the upcoming project and asked them to let their children take the lead in collecting books. I also emphasized that participation was optional, although all the families ultimately contributed. Several families bought brand new books to send, while others sent in boxes of used books. When we had several boxes of books from our own families, I asked the class what we should do to try to get more. They suggested we talk to other classes in our school. Using the ideas from the class, we made posters for the hallways, announced the project in our weekly chapel service, and visited classes on our hallway to talk about the book drive.

When the books started arriving for the book drive, the first graders had to organize themselves to pick them up from the lobby of the school and to deliver them to our classroom. Our classroom was soon overflowing with children's books, and the next task was to pack them successfully into boxes for shipping. I arranged for UPS to come to pick up the cartons of books after the children packed them. While one group of first graders decorated labels for all the books that said "To our pen pals at Rough Rock. Happy reading!," another group glued the labels inside the books. The result of our book drive was nine boxes of donated books, some new and some used, but all of them perfect for a school library that has bare walls and no resources to fill them.

After the books were sent, I asked my students to write in their journals about what they thought it would be like for the Rough Rock students to see our boxes arrive at their school. When everyone was finished, I asked some students to share their writing and pictures with the class. Because community service is required in our K-8 school, my students also drew pictures of what they remembered most from the project to include in their portfolios. We talked as a class about what the children felt they had learned from writing letters and being a pen pal. Later in the year, we received a thank you letter from the principal at Rough Rock. Our pen pals also sent us a class book they had made together, which outlined some of their cultural celebrations and traditions. I read both the letter and the book aloud to my class to bring closure to our project. Many students left first grade with their pen pal's home address so they could write over the summer.

In addition to an address to write to in Arizona, I felt my students were leaving this project with much more. They had all learned to write a coherent letter, though, for many, this was an enormous project that required much adult help. Despite challenges, they all wrote several letters and two postcards to their pen pals in a very short time. They became involved with writing and receiving letters in a way that is different from how they participate in the other monthly community service projects we complete as a class.

Through this project, my students learned about another culture in-depth. They exchanged letters, photographs, drawings, postcards, and art work with children at Rough Rock Community School and through the process, learned how friendships are possible over many miles. My students have also learned that some classes in other schools do not have books lining the walls and do not spend hundreds of dollars on monthly book club offers, but most of all they have gained experience in friendship, in writing, and in giving. For at the heart of this service-learning project, and all of those at our school, is one of the most important lessons for our students to learn, which is that it is in the act of giving that we truly do receive.

For more information about this service-learning project, please contact:
Kate Foley
St. Paul's Episcopal Day School
116 Montecito Avenue
Oakland, California 94610
(510) 433-9797, ext. 17
e-mail: kate_foley@spes.org

AIDS AWARENESS
Robyn Parks
Horace Mann Elementary School, Iowa City, Iowa

SUITABLE GRADE LEVEL(S):   3-6

RELEVANT NCSS STANDARDS:
- **❶ CULTURE**
- **❷ TIME, CONTINUITY, AND CHANGE**
- **❸ PEOPLE, PLACES, AND ENVIRONMENTS**
- **❹ INDIVIDUAL DEVELOPMENT AND IDENTITY**
- **❺ INDIVIDUALS, GROUPS, AND INSTITUTIONS**
- **❽ SCIENCE, TECHNOLOGY, AND SOCIETY**
- **❾ GLOBAL CONNECTIONS**
- **❿ CIVIC IDEALS AND PRACTICES**

SOCIAL STUDIES OBJECTIVES:
1. Increase knowledge of AIDS and its effects in the community.
2. Learn about social services provided for people with HIV/AIDS.
3. Explore the concepts of prejudice and conflict.
4. Use current media sources to learn about current developments with HIV/AIDS in government and health agencies.
5. Create a school community of informed, accepting, and compassionate people.
6. Work to make a difference in the larger community's acceptance of people with HIV/AIDS disease.

PROJECT DESCRIPTION:
I began this service-learning project by contacting our local AIDS support agency, Iowa Center for AIDS Resources and Education (ICARE), to see if they would be willing to have our volunteer support. After receiving a hearty welcome and some possible ways that third graders could contribute to the agency's goals, I went to my building administrator for approval of the project. Because this was my first year in a new building, she filled me in on some recent history, which included the death of a parent from AIDS. The family had been very open with the school, the parents and daughter sharing their experiences as the father was dying from the disease. Once I received administrative support, I wrote a letter home to the parents of my third and fourth graders. I told them my intent regarding the project and asked for their input and support. The next step was to hold a meeting during a September school day with students, interested parents, the building principal, and ICARE director. Although I wanted students to learn more about this disease and the impact it could have on their lives, I did not have a clear agenda as to

how this project would come alive for the students. At the meeting, possible service ideas and questions were presented by all. This meeting set in place the class mission and direction.

The mission of the service-learning project was to raise others' awareness and knowledge of HIV/AIDS and provide support service to ICARE. Activities in the classroom included many opportunities for students to learn, educate others, and provide service to the school and community. The first task for the students was to learn about HIV/AIDS so that they could go out to the other building classrooms and share their information. Trade books were gathered for a reading center and for oral literature time. Some of the titles were *Daddy and Me; Young Arthur Ashe: When Heroes Die; Ryan White: My Own Story; Earthshine; The Eagle Kite; HIV Positive;* and *Understanding AIDS.* Videos and guest speakers from ICARE and the county health department provided additional information about HIV/AIDS. One focus was to learn about where the disease was believed to have originated and spread over time and place. Another focus was on the social services provided to support the disease as well as societal acceptance and nonacceptance. A third focus was placed on health and the standards and values the students would begin to shape and hold regarding people with HIV/AIDS.

Prejudice and conflict became ongoing conversations in the class, beyond the topic of HIV/AIDS. We stayed informed by current media sources (newspapers, magazines, TV, and the Internet) about happenings in government and health agencies, along with local, national, and international stories regarding HIV/AIDS. Using poster pages given to us by ICARE, students colored and crafted a book, *Be a Friend,* to use with preschool and primary age students.

Along with social studies, language arts, and health science curriculum connections, the students completed several math activities for the service-learning project. Students estimated the number of red ribbons they could make from a one-hundred yard spool, how many pins would be needed, and the cost the ribbons would entail. Occasionally the students made ribbons during our weekly service-learning time, but mostly while they were listening to a book read aloud or when their work was finished early. Counting ribbons and pennies were weekly math activities.

During the second year of this project, the county health educator put us in touch with a family who had adopted a young baby who was HIV positive. When the family came to visit the class, the child was five years old and receiving treatment for AIDS. As the family members spoke of their daily experiences, routines, and prejudices they faced, students were pleasantly surprised by how much this kindergarten student was so much like them.

The third graders engaged in a variety of service activities. After approximately three weeks of increasing their knowledge of this disease, students went in small groups to the other classes in the building to present their information and involve them in the project as well. During AIDS Awareness Month (October) and World AIDS Day (December 1), student-made posters were on display on city transit buses, the public library, several local businesses, and the ICARE office. They also put up big red ribbons on the school chain link fence for both of these occasions. Students made red ribbons for distribution at ICARE and other community sites. Student art was printed for thank you cards that ICARE could send to its supporters, volunteers, and other agencies.

Students, with parental support, asked family, friends, and neighbors to give monetary donations to Mother's Voices, a national organization that supports AIDS research. We also became a pen pal support team for two sisters, ages eight and nine, who were HIV positive. We would write letters and send care packages to them and their foster family. This connection was made through The Whitney Project, a peer-based children's HIV/AIDS education project. (The Whitney Project is located at Rural Route 14, Box 203, Santa Fe, New Mexico 87505; phone 505-473-7721.)

Students reflected on their service experiences through writings that were assembled into books, still read in our class today. Students also discussed what they were learning, created interactive bulletin boards, wrote poetry, and made a class quilt. I based my assessments of student learning on their writing, conversations, and interactions with others at work and play. As a teacher, I felt encouraged when hearing students speak about how prejudging could limit their experiences. They were able to use this knowledge as they reflected on how some people reacted to them as they were passing out red ribbons on The University of Iowa campus on World AIDS Day 1995. The lesson the students were learning was one of compassion. Acceptance does not mean endorsement; it is empowerment.

Horace Mann Elementary School students, staff, and parents were very supportive, bringing in pennies for the class penny jars and buying raffle tickets for the quilt that the class had made. The money raised was donated to ICARE. School district nurses, ICARE staff, and the county health office HIV/AIDS educator were supportive and knowledgeable, visiting the class to give information and quick reference needs. We also received financial and practicum student assistance through The University of Iowa's Service-Learning program.

The biggest challenge in carrying out this project was moving past my own fear of how the students and parents might respond initially. Once this fear was put to rest, all seemed relatively easy. There were times when deadlines were short and we pushed to get our work done. It was frustrating for the students that they never heard from the girls or family through The Whitney Project, even though they were told this was a possibility before we began. The Whitney Project did let us know the family was appreciative of what we sent to them. Although the students knew that what they were doing made a difference, the importance of regular face-to-face contact seems to be very important to them, which was difficult to provide. They did, however, enjoy seeing their names and contributions mentioned in the ICARE newsletters and local newspapers.

Two years after this project, it is gratifying to see many of the students select their own service projects in the upper grades that put them directly in touch with people in need: through working with homeless people, free lunch programs, and emergency housing, to name a few. After re-reading the student reflection books, I am aware of their many successes: presenting information to their younger and older peers at school (they were so concerned about how the upper students would receive them), having the support of their parents, having the kindergarten student and her family visit the class, raising money through the penny jars, making the quilt, attending the World AIDS Day celebration on the university campus, having our huge red ribbon banner on the chain link fence left in place without vandalism during October, and making and distributing more than eight thousand red ribbons for AIDS Awareness.

AIDS/HIV awareness is an appropriate student-based, service-learning project that supports many social studies objectives and is easily integrated with several other subject areas as well. This project provided students, parents, and school personnel with the opportunity to become more aware, supportive, and knowledgeable of how the AIDS disease affects all of us.

For further information about this service-learning project, please contact:
Robyn Parks
Horace Mann Elementary School
521 N. Dodge Street
Iowa City, Iowa 52245
phone: (319) 339-6856
e-mail: parks@iowa-city.k12.ia.us

B.I.G.—BRIDGING INTERGENERATIONAL GAPS
Helen Bergey
Perkiomen Valley South Elementary School, Collegeville, Pennsylvania

SUITABLE GRADE LEVEL(S):　　4-6

RELEVANT NCSS STANDARDS:
- **❷ TIME, CONTINUITY, AND CHANGE**
- **❸ PEOPLE, PLACES, AND ENVIRONMENTS**
- **❹ INDIVIDUAL DEVELOPMENT AND IDENTITY**
- **❿ CIVIC IDEALS AND PRACTICES**

SOCIAL STUDIES OBJECTIVES:
1. Develop an understanding of regions of the United States through learning about what it was like to grow up in different parts of the country.

2. Discover the influence that previous generations have had on the history of the United States.

3. Understand the concepts of workplace and marketplace and learn how both have changed over time.

PROJECT DESCRIPTION:

Bridging Intergenerational Gaps was a service-learning project that paired 135 fourth grade students at Perkiomen Valley South Elementary School in Collegeville, Pennsylvania, with senior citizens to gather oral histories. In addition, the students constructed multiple intelligence projects to tell the story of their interviews. As the instructional support teacher and volunteer coordinator in my elementary building of K-5 students, I saw the special relationship that developed between senior citizen volunteers and students that they tutored. I also was aware of how our society's transient nature has sometimes deprived our students of the wisdom that is available from senior members of society. At times, I encountered negative attitudes toward aging on the part of the students. In addition to the social studies objectives outlined above, I wanted students to appreciate senior citizens as important members of society while learning history firsthand. I wanted senior citizens to feel a sense of belonging to the youth in our school and to feel that their ideas and experiences were valued.

Preparation for the B.I.G. project began in the spring when a group of six third grade students with diverse ethnic backgrounds, gender, and ability were selected to be on the Student Planning Committee. I told them that the project, which was being planned for the following school year, would include having fourth grade students collect an oral history from a senior citizen and then create a multiple intelligence project to enhance their written report. The students chose a name for the project and helped set timelines for the following year. Their input was used in applying for a Robinson Mini Grant from The Constitutional Rights Foundation. We received the grant, although we would have carried out the project anyway because of the enthusiasm that was building. The additional funds helped us purchase disposable cameras, supplies, and treats for the celebration at the end of the project.

I met with the classroom teachers in September to explain what had been done so far and to get their input on the next steps for the project. As a group, we decided to allow the Student Planning Committee to continue to guide the project. Each of the five fourth grade teachers was enthusiastic and supportive, helping with the organization and logistics, as well as assisting individual students to adhere to the appropriate timelines.

The Student Planning Committee met early in the fall to brainstorm questions to be used on the pre- and post-attitude surveys such as "How old is old?" and "In what kinds of activities do 'old' people participate?" The interview questions were brainstormed and refined, and the committee listed possible multiple intelligence projects. The students on the committee were also responsible for explaining the B.I.G. project to the students in their respective classrooms. After the pre-project attitude surveys were completed in school and returned, the interview questions were distributed. It was explained that these questions were to serve as a guide rather than to be strictly adhered to. Disposable cameras were available in each classroom for the students to borrow, with encouragement to take a picture of their senior. Later on in the project, students used these pictures in the Hyperstudio stacks as well as in a collage of students and seniors.

Almost all of the fourth graders independently located a senior citizen to interview. Teachers paired the few students who were unable to find someone with a senior volunteer or community member. After the interviews were completed, students shared their reports within each classroom. Then a notebook was created containing all 135 oral histories. Thus, students learned from each of the oral histories shared within their classrooms and also had the opportunity to read the histories completed by students in the other classes.

Students learned about seniors who had diverse childhoods and who lived in many different parts of the country. Fourth graders were interested to learn about toys, leisure time, prices of candy and soda, and favorite teachers from another generation. They compared similarities and differences between their seniors' lives and their own lives.

The next step was to complete multiple intelligence projects. Students were given the date when projects would be completed in school. We let students know that they could bring materials from home or use the materials available at school. When project day arrived, all fourth grade classes worked at the same time. Special area teachers and classroom aides provided support for students needing extra guidance. Projects included posters, picture albums, Hyperstudio stacks, timelines, dioramas, stitchery, memorabilia collections, songs, collages, and audio and video recordings. Every single fourth grader completed an oral history and a project! As the facilitator of B.I.G., the project seemed to be an easy task to accomplish, but I am aware that the classroom teachers were instrumental when deadlines were approaching. Built-in check points ensured that no student would be without a senior to interview or without materials for the project. An enthusiastic building principal was an asset as well.

Students made many connections between the B.I.G. project and the social studies curriculum. As students were studying regions and climates of the United States, they developed an awareness about the impact that living in different regions had on the previous generation's childhoods, day-to-day life, and choices of careers and vocations. Students enhanced their map skills as they located where their senior citizens had lived. As students wrote individual reports on states and cooperative group reports on regions, they could make real life connections in terms of climate, history, and geography.

The seniors helped make history come alive for these elementary students. Students compared transportation, inventions, scientific discoveries, medical advances, and technology in the present to the past. Some of the seniors had been in the military and explained firsthand the impact that the Korean and Vietnam Wars had on them and the United States. Several of the seniors had lived through the Depression and talked about the hardships they experienced during that period of our nation's history. Students also heard about ethnic neighborhoods, traditions, and values that developed within close-knit communities that are not as prevalent today.

Many of the seniors talked about growing up on farms and in small industrial towns. Students were able to see how the numbers of farms have diminished over time and how the farming industry has been changed by advanced technology. Some seniors talked about people migrating to sections of the country where jobs were available. Even the comparison of simple items such as candy bar prices or types of common toys provided students with interesting history lessons.

In addition to social studies, curriculum integration included reading because fourth grade literature focuses on friendships and intergenerational themes, math to compile a list of prices of goods then and now, and language arts where writing and oral interviewing skills were enhanced. Students also used their musical, artistic, and computer skills when constructing their multiple intelligence projects.

At the end of the project, we organized an Intergenerational Celebration for students, their parents, and the senior citizens who were interviewed. Those attending viewed a slide presentation using a student-created *Hyperstudio* stack detailing the project, and they looked at the projects displayed in the school lobby. Through displaying the projects around the school, the entire student body and faculty were able to view the projects. (We reached an even larger audience through an article in the local newspaper). We also served refreshments and invited the senior citizens to comment on the B.I.G. project on large poster paper that was available. These comments served as their reflections of the project.

Students reflected on their learning and changes in attitude by completing the post-project attitude survey forms. Evidence of changes in students' attitudes can be seen in their responses to the following question: What kinds of activities do "old" people participate in? On the pre-surveys, typical responses included clean, watch TV, play cards, sit in a wheelchair, sit down a lot, sleep, knit, play Bingo, eat mashed foods, go to casinos, read the newspaper, and play board games. Contrast these ideas with students' responses to the same question after the project. They wrote: ride a bike, shop, sing in the choir, travel, play sports, volunteer, whatever they like to do; some simply have fun; they can do anything; drive a car at a low speed limit; there is no limit to being old; some are very active; play with grandchildren, and go to shows. Both the surveys and the seniors' reflections on poster paper helped students reflect further in class discussions.

In addition to compiling the pre- and post-attitude surveys and the interviews into notebooks, we created a scrapbook to detail the positive journey through the generations that our fourth graders took. A copy of the scrapbook was presented to the Constitutional Rights Foundation as a "thank you"!

Both senior citizens and the students learned a lot from each other during the course of the B.I.G. project. This service-learning project made fourth grade social studies "come alive"! Additionally, students and senior citizens gained a positive understanding of another generation. By increasing the interaction between the generations, a true celebration of age took place at Perkiomen Valley South Elementary School!

For more information about this service-learning project, please contact:
Helen Bergey
Perkiomen Valley South Elementary School
200 East Third Avenue
Trapp, PA 19426
phone: (610)-489-2991
e-mail: hbergey@mciunix.mciu.k12.pa.us

MARINE ENVIRONMENTAL ACTIVISM

Gerri Faivre

East Woods School, Oyster Bay, New York

SUITABLE GRADE LEVEL(S):   3-6

RELEVANT NCSS STANDARDS:

- **Ⅱ TIME, CONTINUITY, AND CHANGE**
- **Ⅲ PEOPLE, PLACES, AND ENVIRONMENTS**
- **Ⅴ INDIVIDUALS, GROUPS, AND INSTITUTIONS**
- **Ⅵ POWER, AUTHORITY, AND GOVERNANCE**
- **Ⅸ GLOBAL CONNECTIONS**
- **Ⅹ CIVIC IDEALS AND PRACTICES**

SOCIAL STUDIES OBJECTIVES:

1. Learn about the problems and challenges involved in working to remedy a contemporary environmental issue (e.g., marine life).

2. Use facts and persuasive writing in letters to government officials, newspapers, and organizations working on behalf of marine life.

3. Understand the connections between local and global problems related to marine life.

4. Learn about a variety of different civic actions that can make a difference (e.g., letters, petitions, public presentations, direct action, personal life-style).

5. Identify and participate in both governmental and nongovernmental efforts to preserve marine life.

6. Explore the historical aspects of the problems confronting marine life today.

7. Recognize the role of the media in promoting public awareness and changes in public policy.

8. Learn how a bill becomes a law in the U. S. government.

PROJECT DESCRIPTION:

In spring 1985, I read an article in the Long Island newspaper about an interdisciplinary, multimedia pilot program called "The Voyage of the Mimi."[1] That summer East Woods School purchased the Mimi program on my recommendation. The program included a miniseries on videotape based on the old salt Captain Granville and his six-member crew on a summer long whale tracking expedition in the Gulf of Maine, as well as computer software, lesson materials, laboratory projects, and a newsletter.

Between 1985 and 1988, my fifth grade students' interest in whales and all marine mammals, oceanography, and other related marine science matters grew out of projects connected with The Voyage of the Mimi. New materials were added to the course of study, and a schoolwide Marine Week was instituted.

By 1987, the cross-curricular aspects of the Mimi project really began to take hold. A three day field trip to Boston, Salem, and Gloucester, Massachusetts, combined elements of English, history, and science. In addition, math classes studied nautical time, latitude and longitude, and charting. In science, a study of the effects of acid rain on marine life was added to the curriculum. Current events interest increased as newspaper clippings and magazine articles about marine mammals streamed into the classroom.

The students were now also becoming authors and political activists on behalf of all cetaceans. The fifth graders wrote a "Kidsday" section of Long Island's *Newsday* newspaper with articles about saving the whales and protesting the slaughter of whales by Denmark and Japan.

In fall 1987, two sixth graders read an article in *Science World* magazine about a proposed island casino to be built in the middle of Stellwagen Bank, the main feeding grounds for humpback whales in the Gulf of Maine. Outraged by this proposal, the students brought it to my attention, and I encouraged them to take action. The two students formulated a petition, which they had signed by all members of the East Woods community. They also circulated the petition throughout the immediate geographical area and sent copies to other teachers throughout the United States whom I had met on research expeditions during the summer months. Petitions were also sent to the National Marine Fisheries Bureau and to both the Bush and Dukakis campaign.

The petition committed East Woods to the preservation of the environment and to the plight of cetaceans, and strongly protested the proposal for a 155 acre island casino in the Gulf of Maine. Four major impacts to the environment were clearly described within the petition, which ultimately gathered several thousand signatures. The students received many letters from other students in the fifty states agreeing with their position on the island casino and indicating that they too had taken up the cause. So far, public opinion has been successful; to date, no such island casino exists in the Gulf of Maine.

During the early spring of 1988, fifth grade students read an ad in the *New York Times* regarding the killing of 150,000 dolphins in tuna nets. The children were shocked by this, and many began convincing their parents to boycott the sale of tuna fish. They also requested that the kitchen staff refrain from serving tuna at school. Although this could not be accomplished totally, the students were able to provide alternative food choices to tuna fish for students who wished to abstain in support of the dolphins. Also, kitchen staff agreed to purchase only tuna caught on line; this agreement was documented in writing to the fifth graders.

At the same time, what would become a several-year letter-writing campaign began. The first group of letters was mailed to Mr. David Brower of Earth Island Institute in San Francisco, California. Mr. Brower forwarded the students' letters to Gerry E. Studds, then chairman of the House of Representatives Subcommittee on Fisheries, Wildlife Conservation, and the Environment. The renewal of the Marine Mammals Protection Act was up for a vote that year, and the goal was to bring the killing of dolphins down to zero. In a reply from Mr. Studds, the students were thanked for their concern and action, and encouraged to keep up their involvement.

Our service-learning efforts also involved direct action. By the winter of 1989, East Woods students had participated in several beach clean up days on the north shore, where the school is located. In January, the students spent a Saturday braving the cold on the south shore beaches and placing old Christmas trees in a diamond shape to help catch the sand and reinforce the dunes, thereby preventing their erosion. The students also collected more than two hundred pounds of debris from the beach. The event was covered by the local media, and an East Woods student was quoted as saying, "I am doing something to help my children's future."

At the same time, an environmental committee of students, parents, and faculty had been formed to prepare for The Environmental Expo to be held in May, culminating a year-long emphasis on environmental awareness throughout the school. East Woods was also working closely with The Whaling Museum in Cold Spring Harbor to coordinate activities that would enhance the fifth grade curriculum and help prepare the children for their three day trip to Mystic Seaport, with a focus on the history of whaling and life in a seaport community. The Whaling Museum has provided many enriching and educational moments for East Woods students over the ensuing years. East Woods students have since spoken at the Whaling Museum several times based on their extended field studies in Florida and Canada as they pursued their education on the environment and marine mammals. They have also spoken at a New York State Marine Educators Student Conference and at the Youth Can Conference in New York City.

In July 1989, I received a letter from Robins Barstow, Executive Director of the Cetacean Society International, indicating that Representative Barbara Boxer of California had just introduced in the U.S. Congress a proposed bill, H. R. 2926, The Dolphin Protection Consumer Information Act of 1989. Mr. Barstow indicated to me that the letters the students had forwarded to him the previous spring had been sent directly to Representative Boxer. The letters would be highly effective in garnering support for H. R. 2926 and would be read on the floor of Congress. The fifth grade students also received a citation from the Cetacean Society International in recognition of their extraordinary letter writing effort to save dolphins dying in tuna nets. The children were validated beyond all expectations! The U.S. Government had listened and had understood what they were saying, and because of the efforts of the students, the government was going to try and do something to solve the problem. They had truly made a difference. One student wrote directly to Barbara Boxer and received a personal response explaining in-depth the details of HR 2926.

During the 1989-90 academic year, the social studies classes paid particular attention to how a bill becomes a law, focusing on the progress of HR 2926. Representative Boxer kept in close contact with us regarding the labeling of dolphin-safe tuna, which would allow consumers a significant voice in setting environmental policy. When the bill was passed by Congress, East Woods School received public recognition by Newsday and CBS radio for being instrumental in helping to convince major tuna corporations to refuse tuna that were caught in nets set on dolphins.

In the meantime, East Woods was busy planning the Marine Environment Expo for the spring of 1990. In May, more than 2,500 students from twenty-six Long Island schools were welcomed to the expo, co-chaired by a parent, Jamie Deming, and me. The Mimi, a seventy-two foot ketch, was the center of the expo, the culmination of a five year effort to involve children in environmental concerns and demonstrate to them that everyone can be part of stemming the destruction of the natural world. The children of East Woods School, who had long embraced the study of the marine environment prior to the expo, published the *Marine Environment Handbook*, a hardcover guide to many marine science topics, to help sponsor the event.

Our service-learning project on behalf of marine mammals continues to grow. As a result of the publicity about our school, we were selected by the Dolphin Research Center on Grassy Key, Florida, to assist in the establishment of an environmental education program for youth. In March 1999, East Woods will send its thirteenth Dolphin Research Center Team to Florida. More than 225 students and forty-five faculty members have participated in the program since its inception. Our students and faculty get an honest, in-depth look at pure marine mammal research and the environmental impact on our oceans. East Woods' commitment to environmental concerns has encouraged many of our former students to pursue the marine and environmental sciences in secondary school, knowing that this choice will lead them to college courses in the same field of interest, and perhaps a career choice as well.

Thirteen years have gone by since the beginning of The Voyage of the Mimi at East Woods School. The civic involvement, service-learning, and educational activities that have developed out of students' interest in the curriculum have helped to make East Woods students terrestrial ambassadors for the marine environment as they continue to speak out on its behalf, trying to make a difference while encouraging the rest of the world to do the same.

For more information about this service-learning project, please contact:
Gerri Faivre
East Woods School
31 Yellow Cote Road
Oyster Bay, New York 11771
phone: 516-922-4400, ext. 313
fax: 516-922-2589

Notes
1. Bank Street College of Education, *The Voyage of the Mimi*. Pleasantville, N.Y.: Sunburst Communication. 1985

CHAPTER 3

SERVICE-LEARNING PROJECTS FOR MIDDLE SCHOOL SOCIAL STUDIES

Middle school students, as emerging adolescents, want opportunities to exercise their independence and make their own choices. The stories in this chapter show how service-learning projects can empower early adolescents to make significant decisions that affect their learning and the well-being of their communities. Richard Bradley and Kim Rhodes write about how middle class eighth graders confronted the challenging social issue of homelessness, and related it to both their own lives and social studies units on The Great Depression and the United States Constitution. Michele Cerino tells how she connected her middle schoolers with local and state lawmakers to get involved with the political process by advocating for services for people with AIDS. In Diane Vliem's social studies class, issues related to hunger chosen by students led to persuasive speeches given to businesses and social service agencies. Finally, Deb Bradley writes about the lessons her student leaders learned about community planning and city government regulations through advocating the construction of a new school playground. These middle school students, while challenged by the complexity of social issues and government politics, learned that persistence pays off in making a difference.

POVERTY AND HOMELESSNESS: THE OPEN SHELTER PROJECT

L. Richard Bradley
Columbus, Ohio
Kim Rhodes
Jones Middle School, Upper Arlington, Ohio

SUITABLE GRADE LEVEL(S): 5-8

RELEVANT NCSS STANDARDS:

- **❶ CULTURE**
- **Ⓘⓥ INDIVIDUAL DEVELOPMENT AND IDENTITY**
- **Ⓥ INDIVIDUALS, GROUPS, AND INSTITUTIONS**
- **Ⓥ️Ⓘ POWER, AUTHORITY, AND GOVERNANCE**
- **Ⓥ️Ⓘ️Ⓘ PRODUCTION, DISTRIBUTION, AND CONSUMPTION**
- **Ⓘ️Ⓧ GLOBAL CONNECTIONS**
- **Ⓧ CIVIC IDEALS AND PRACTICES**

SOCIAL STUDIES OBJECTIVES:

1. See the world from the perspectives of those who are homeless.

2. Learn about the reasons that people become homeless, the impact of poverty on people's lives, and what people living in poverty do to cope with their circumstances.

3. Think critically about a social issue (homelessness).

4. Explore the role that local government departments play in relation to a homeless shelter.

PROJECT DESCRIPTION:

Service-learning projects related to poverty and homelessness are part of the educational mission of Jones Middle School. Sixth grade teams work with a child care center for low-income families; seventh graders work with the Homeless Families Foundation. The focus of this article is the eighth grade's partnership with the Open Shelter.

The goal of the Jones Open Shelter Project is to involve students in a service-learning activity that helps them better understand the causes of poverty and homelessness. This project, which began ten years ago, grew out of a teacher's desire to find a better way to teach her students the concepts contained in a social studies unit about "Poverty and the Great Depression." A primary focus of the Open Shelter project is to enable young people who have grown up in an upper-middle class, white suburban community to experience what it is like to be part of another world—a world in which people are poor and often homeless. Rather than simply talk about the differences, this project enables students to see the world from another perspective by reflecting on the stories and experiences of the men they meet at the shelter. Activities at the shelter put young people in situations that challenge them to think about who they are and what they think about issues such as homelessness. Through their interactions with shelter residents, students learn about the real reasons people become homeless, the impact of poverty on people's lives, and what those who are poor do to try to cope.

The Open Shelter, located just west of downtown Columbus, Ohio, serves a diversified male population. The average length of stay at the shelter is about thirty days. Residents of the shelter differ racially, in geographic background, in abilities (some have disabilities), and in nationality, thus exposing students to a wide range of beliefs, values, and traditions. Many come from foreign countries and are in the United States legally but have run into career-related difficulties. Language barriers are often a problem in identifying and serving the needs of these residents. Sometimes students in the program are able to use their school language skills to help shelter staff in translating.

The project begins in December, with students taking a pre-test on their knowledge of and attitudes toward homelessness and poverty. Then they watch a video on homelessness and write in their journals on the question "What homelessness means to me ...." They also sponsor a schoolwide drive to collect personal hygiene items on the men's "Wish List." These are assembled into bags, gift-wrapped, and delivered prior to the school's winter break. There is also a briefing for parents so that they have a better understanding of what the project will involve.

In January, the director of the Open Shelter meets with students at the school to talk about the shelter and what they are likely to see and experience. The director gives the students information about the history and purpose of the Open Shelter. He also asks them to think about the possible reasons why a shelter might be needed in our society and why it is located where it is, instead of out in the suburbs. The teacher asks students to discuss the following question with their parents: "How would you feel about having a group home in your neighborhood?" The director and the teacher also lead the students in a role play about what it would be like to live on a welfare budget. The teacher also shows slides of the shelter to the students and has an orientation meeting with parent volunteers so that all participants will have some idea of what they will see when they get there.

During the months of January, February, and March, students visit the shelter weekly, riding public transportation. While at the shelter, they interact with residents and help them in a variety of ways. Service activities include cleaning lockers, sorting and hanging donated clothing, unloading trucks (e.g., mattresses), cleaning the grounds around the shelter, arranging food on the shelves in the storage room, stuffing envelopes for mailings, sweeping and mopping floors, folding bedding, stacking chairs, emptying trash, and serving the meal. All of these activities are done alongside residents, giving students a chance to interact. Students also have a period of time focused more specifically on conversing with the residents, who typically encourage them to stay in school, study hard, stay away from drugs and alcohol, and make good decisions. Students with computer skills have also been helping residents at the shelter learn how to use computers. Each resident has his own e-mail address, which he uses for job interviews.

Several sources of support help to facilitate this project. Funding initially came from Learn & Serve America minigrants of up to $500, but now comes from other sources within the Upper Arlington School District. Parents are also an important source of support for the shelter activities. Some transport food for the meal that students prepare and serve at the shelter. Others supervise work groups at the shelter, working alongside students and residents. These shared experiences enable parents and their children to develop special relationships built on mutual service to others.

The Jones Open Shelter Project is part of a social studies unit on "Poverty and the Great Depression." The unit begins with students viewing a video titled "No Place Like Home." Students then take a survey on their attitudes about homelessness in Franklin County. The survey asks students to reflect on how often and where they see people they think might be homeless, why they might be homeless, what services are needed for homeless people, and who should provide these services. Because they ride public transportation to and from the shelter, students also discuss the importance of mass transportation in cities and learn how bus routes can limit where homeless people can work. (In Columbus, for example, there are no bus routes outside the "outer belt." However, this is where most of the new jobs are being created.) Students are continually encouraged to connect what they are learning with their own lives, for example, through an assignment to discuss with their parents the following question: How long would our family be able to sustain our current way of life if one or both parents lost their job?

As part of another social studies unit on the United States Constitution, students learn about the functions of the various departments of the government and what each branch does in relation to the needs of the men they meet at the shelter. They learn about the specific role the Department of Housing and Human Development plays in providing assistance for shelters across the country. They also learn how decisions made at the local level influence where shelter facilities will be located, who will be served, and what other services will be offered.

Language arts skills are used in journal writing, and the preparation of final reports and presentations. Students write poetry after they have visited the shelter and short stories about how people become homeless. In addition, once they begin the project, students often choose books to read for their language arts classes that relate to poverty and homelessness. Students also plan and prepare a meal at the shelter with assistance from the family and consumer science staff at the school.

Reflection is an ongoing process throughout the project. Students are required to keep journals that are read regularly by the social studies and language arts teachers. Reflection also occurs immediately following each trip to the shelter when students get back to school. This is a time for students to reveal their true feelings (which range from pity to guilt) about what they are experiencing. At the conclusion of the project, students do a final reflective piece that illustrates what they have learned. Over the years, these have included stories, photo essays, songs, poetry, and presentations to peers and city officials. Students are also given post-tests (using the same survey as at the beginning of the project) on their knowledge of and attitudes about homelessness and poverty.

Through their experiences at the shelter, students become very aware of how much "stuff" middle class people waste. As they work side by side with homeless men sorting donated clothing, many are also surprised to find out that these people still have some pride and have feelings. They wouldn't accept these torn and tattered clothes for themselves; why should homeless people be expected to be grateful? They also learn that becoming homeless is something that could happen to anyone. Another question the teacher asks students to discuss with their parents illustrates this: "If, suddenly, there was no income coming in, how long could our family continue living the way we do?"

As students become more aware of the reasons people become homeless, they also become more aware of the interconnectedness of the global economy and what that means for employment opportunities for unskilled and semiskilled workers in the United States. They are also more aware of the fact that homelessness is not just a problem in our society but in many other parts of the world as well.

There have been several challenges in facilitating the Open Shelter project. When the program first began ten years ago, it did not have the support of the school administrators. Once they heard students talking about the impact the project had on them, however, they got behind it. Each year, a few parents refuse to sign the permission slips to allow their children to participate. Sometimes the weather is a problem, but the teacher chose the months of January-March to emphasize the fact that homelessness is a year-round problem and not just something we think about from Thanksgiving to Christmas.

Being involved in the Open Shelter project has had a visible impact on student participants. One result of these interactions is that 90 percent of the students have reported increases in self-confidence, competence, and self-awareness, coupled with greater acceptance of cultural diversity. Another is that students are better able to think critically about and discuss other social issues. Pre- to post-differences on the "Perceptions of the Homeless" survey typically show reduced use of stereotypes and a heightened awareness of the problems of poverty and homelessness in the greater Columbus area. As measured by the "Checklist of Personal Gains," students show more positive attitudes toward poor and homeless people (90 percent); have an increased awareness of the real causes of poverty and homelessness (90 percent); and feel a sense of usefulness in relation to the community and a sense of responsibility for doing "something" to help (80 percent), because they see homelessness as "everyone's problem."

Additionally, when these students go on to high school, they are better prepared and more willing to be involved in and support activities that reflect their commitments. "Alumni" of the Open Shelter Project initially came up with the idea of the Upper Arlington School District working with Habitat for Humanity in some way. Their enthusiasm quickly spread to administrators, teachers, parents, and their peers—the result being a first-of-its-kind partnership between a school district and Habitat. This districtwide project involves students from all grade levels, culminating in a new home for a low-income family. Other "alumni," now in college, have told their teacher that they selected careers in social work or psychology because of their experiences at the Open Shelter.

For many students, the Open Shelter project is an eye-opening experience that gives them a hands-on experience of active citizenship. Not only are students more aware of problems in their community, they also are learning the skills necessary to be part of the solution. Whether the issue is poverty and homelessness or pollution of a local river, the students are developing a commitment to making a positive difference in their world.

For more information about this service-learning project, please contact:

Richard Bradley, Ph.D.
6489 Brookbend Drive
Columbus, Ohio 43235–5001
phone: (614) 793-9758
e-mail: bradley.16@osu.edu

Ms. Kim Rhodes
Jones Middle School
2100 Arlington Avenue
Upper Arlington, Ohio 43221
phone: (614) 487-5080

ACTION, ADVOCACY, AND AIDS
Michele Cerino
West Hills Middle Magnet School, New Haven, Connecticut

SUITABLE GRADE LEVEL(S): 6-8

RELEVANT NCSS STANDARDS:

- **Ⓘ INDIVIDUAL DEVELOPMENT AND IDENTITY**
- **Ⓥ INDIVIDUALS, GROUPS, AND INSTITUTIONS**
- **Ⓥ POWER, AUTHORITY, AND GOVERNANCE**
- **Ⓧ CIVIC IDEALS AND PRACTICES**

SOCIAL STUDIES OBJECTIVES:

1. Describe the three branches of the U.S. government.
2. Explain the legislative process of the U.S. government.
3. Research and analyze the U.S. government's response to AIDS-related issues.
4. Apply citizen's initiative by proposing and lobbying for AIDS-related reform.

PROJECT DESCRIPTION:

"Action, Advocacy, and AIDS" is a comprehensive, integrated unit that addresses social development, human sexuality, government policy, and the writing process through the study of the legislative branch of the U.S. government. The topic of HIV/AIDS is highly emotional and controversial from a public, political, and educational viewpoint, evoking deep discussion and high motivation in adolescent and teenage youth. This project has special significance in the urban setting because AIDS is spreading in epidemic proportions in minority populations. This project gives students a unique opportunity to make a huge impact in their own community, while learning valuable lessons in citizenship, leadership, and personal responsibility.

"Action, Advocacy, and AIDS" has four main components: research, activism, peer education, and community service. Preparation begins with structured lessons about the three branches of government with an emphasis on the legislative branch. Students then conduct research to identify local and state politicians, their views, and current proposed legislation. Using a Connecticut State Legislature guide and maps of New Haven neighborhoods, students identify aldermen from their own wards and representatives and senators from their district. Then students write letters to these politicians, stating their views on AIDS related issues and asking for a response.

Students collect information from a variety of sources including current periodicals, the Internet, brochures, and government-produced materials (e.g., The Connecticut Legislative Guide). Concurrently, students are learning about HIV/AIDS (using library resources, AIDS organization-produced materials, videos, and HIV positive speakers) and persuasive writing techniques.

During small- and large-group discussions, students identify areas of interest such as the Needle Exchange Program, AIDS in minority groups, and peer education programs. An advocacy letter-writing campaign develops as students identify problems and search for solutions. This campaign usually results in personal meetings with the mayor, local and state lawmakers, and other officials. Often, students are contacted and asked to work on areas of concern. For example, in 1996, New Haven Mayor DeStefano asked students to write letters to Connecticut senators in order to defeat a proposed bill that would end funding for Needle Exchange Programs (NEP). When the bill was defeated, the mayor then requested that students write letters to Senator Toni Harp to thank her for her diligence in working to defeat the NEP bill. All students participating in this project were made honorary members of the Mayor's Task Force on AIDS.

In both years that this project has been conducted, students have identified a theme or particular concern on which to focus. In 1996, students worked to keep the NEP alive. They also identified the need for more educational materials for both Spanish-speaking and illiterate people. The Mayor's Task Force asked the group to construct an information center at the main public library. It included information for children and adults in English and Spanish, and featured posters that presented prevention messages in pictures.

In 1997, students worked to gain funding and establish middle school peer education programs. Students followed their letter-writing campaign with e-mail and phone calls to set up appointments with lawmakers. On March 9, 1998, Connecticut AIDS Awareness Day, students met with Senators Harp and Crisco and Representatives Dyson and DePino to enlist their support. They also spoke with other Connecticut activists on an information panel. In June 1998, the Mayor's Task Force invited students to speak at a State Board of Education hearing against limiting guidelines for Health and Human Sexuality curricula. The students' impassioned speeches helped sway the board to establish comprehensive and explicit curriculum guidelines, despite strong conservative opponents.

Students also plan peer education activities. An information center is created in the school's front hall, and games are conducted in other classrooms. For example, the students play the game "Transmission," in which each student is given a bag of colored candy and told to exchange one piece with as many others as he or she chooses. Students are not told that the two green candy pieces represent HIV. The two students who hold green candies at the end of the game are told that they have contracted AIDS, and the two who started with the green pieces are responsible for the transmission. Anyone else who exchanged with any of these four students is told that he or she may have contracted HIV. On most occasions when this simulation is played, the only totally safe students are those who chose to abstain from exchanging candy pieces with everyone else.

Another game we often play is called "Values and Choices." The classroom is divided into three areas marked "Agree," "Disagree," and "Unsure." Then, statements such as "I would be afraid to hug someone with HIV" are read aloud and students move to the area of the room that best represents their feelings to the statement. This activity is a great starting point for discussion and journal writing about students' attitudes regarding HIV and AIDS.

Finally, students plan and implement service projects based on genuine community needs, such as "adopting" and visiting the Leeway House (a residence for adults living with AIDS); serving as members of the New Haven Task Force on AIDS; participating in a candlelight vigil on World AIDS day; and creating and selling informational bookmarks to raise funds for children affected by AIDS. Students identify these service opportunities by contacting all AIDS organizations through letters and phone calls. Other service activities that students have completed include baking cookies and making holiday gifts for residents of the Leeway House, conducting bake sales, selling ribbons on World AIDS Day, and soliciting toy donations for AIDS-affected children during the winter holidays. This past holiday season, students hand-sewed forty stockings, filled them with treats, and delivered them to the Leeway House. Students also raised $100 for toys and helped with preparations for World AIDS Day on the New Haven Green. Most importantly, students are a strong and active voice in the school and community, and at home and church, for AIDS prevention and compassion education.

Evaluation can be difficult; it is not easy to measure personal and emotional growth through traditional quantitative methods. Authentic assessments such as weekly reflection journals and holistically scored writing pieces are used as well as standard social studies tests. I am currently developing data-based assessments using the following information: pre-service and post-service questionnaires, number of times each student participates in service activities, and feedback from the school and community.

Despite challenges such as lack of funding, costly transportation, and lack of schoolwide teacher support (too time-consuming, too controversial), students and their supportive parents continue to participate enthusiastically and enjoy numerous successes. My students' relentless pursuit of educational, political, and social reform associated with AIDS has resulted in the continuation of the New Haven Needle Exchange program and the construction of a teen information center at the New Haven public library. They successfully testified at a State Board of Education hearing for explicit and comprehensive sexuality standards for middle school curriculum (despite vehement protests from a vocal, conservative parent group). Also, by enlisting the support of lawmakers, the mayor, and every AIDS organization in New Haven, students persuaded the superintendent of schools to finance peer education at West Hills Middle School for the next three years as a pilot program for possible districtwide implementation.

The most overwhelming accomplishments to me are the ones that cannot be precisely measured and are best described by my students in their own words.

> I thought this was going to be just any old project. I learned that this is serious and interesting and is the best (thing) I ever did because we might save many lives. – *Josue, age 11*

> There are things that maybe I would have done if I didn't learn these things this year. This project changed my life forever. – *Ismael, age 11*

> The most important thing we can do is educate people. –*LaDonna, age 12*

I'm thinking about a career in government. This project helped me learn about the legislative process firsthand. — *Justin, age 14*

AIDS is the number one cause of death for African American women. As a young African American woman, I am concerned. —*Allyse, age 14*

My students know that regardless of race, age, or socioeconomic status, they have made a difference. They have actively participated in the democratic ideal as compassionate, caring citizens and it has changed them forever.

For more information about this service-learning project, please contact:
Michele Cerino
West Hills Middle Magnet School
103 Hallock Avenue
New Haven, Connecticut 06519
phone: (203) 946-8279

THE HUNGER PROJECT
Diane Vliem
Moore Middle School, Jefferson County Schools, Colorado

SUITABLE GRADE LEVEL(S): 7-8

RELEVANT NCSS STANDARDS:
- **Ⅰ** **CULTURE**
- **Ⅱ** **TIME, CONTINUITY, AND CHANGE**
- **Ⅲ** **PEOPLE, PLACES, AND ENVIRONMENTS**
- **Ⅳ** **INDIVIDUAL DEVELOPMENT AND IDENTITY**
- **Ⅴ** **INDIVIDUALS, GROUPS, AND INSTITUTIONS**
- **Ⅵ** **POWER, AUTHORITY, AND GOVERNANCE**
- **Ⅹ** **CIVIC IDEALS AND PRACTICES**

SOCIAL STUDIES OBJECTIVES:
1. Explain a contemporary issue (e.g., hunger) using geographic knowledge, skills, and perspectives.

2. Explain which level of government students should contact to express opinions or get help with specific problems.

3. Describe ways in which nongovernmental organizations have sought to help solve the problem.

4. Recognize that government policies have consequences for individuals, groups, and organizations in the community.

5. Evaluate, take, and defend positions on the importance of civic responsibilities to the individual and to society.

6. Identify means by which citizens can monitor and influence the formation and implementation of public policy.

PROJECT DESCRIPTION:

Four teachers at our middle school chose the theme of hunger for an interdisciplinary unit involving social studies, language arts, math, and science. We received a grant in 1996 from Goals 2000 with additional funding from Active Citizenship Today to develop an integrated service-learning project that would meet standards in the four subject areas. We piloted the unit during the 1996-97 school year; the following year two of the teachers were reassigned to other teams. Our continuing service-learning collaboration, now in its third year, focuses on social studies and language arts.

The current project involves students learning about the issue of hunger, globally and locally, and then choosing a service-learning activity that addresses an identified aspect of the problem. Using a teacher-created handbook, students are guided through several steps including researching hunger in the local community, identifying community agencies that focus on hunger, and brainstorming possible ways they can help address unmet needs. For the service aspect of the project, each student develops a brochure and a persuasive speech and then shares these with an individual, business, or organization in the community that he or she hopes to involve in the effort to address community food-related problems. Examples of topics students have selected include food wasting in stores and restaurants, high fat content in fast food restaurants or school cafeterias, problems with food delivery to elderly persons or people with disabilities, medical food disorders such as anorexia and bulimia, safety problems in soup kitchens, and food spoilage. Students are also encouraged to complete extra credit options, which include working at a soup kitchen, delivering meals to the homebound, or writing to a national or worldwide organization that is working on hunger-related concerns (e.g., Oxfam, CARE, Salvation Army, Red Cross).

Several published curriculum materials have been useful in preparing and guiding the students to complete these activities. First, *Global Geography System, Geographic Inquiry into Global Issues: Hunger* gives students a global perspective on the study of their community food-related problems.[1] A video, "Hidden in America" (available at video rental stores), educates students on hunger in the United States. Finally, the Active Citizenship Today (ACT) *Student Handbook* provides a useful framework for students to include the essential elements of service-learning in their projects.[2]

The service-learning unit begins by giving each student a binder of necessary materials. These include letters that students can distribute to parents and community members explaining the project and three color coded sections: (1) Planning and Organizing the Project, (2) Brochure and Speech Tasks, and (3) Reflection and Poster Night. This binder is brought to language arts and social studies classes every day until it is turned in completed; each section is described in greater detail below.

Completing Section One of the binder involves three tasks. First, students do research and brainstorming to develop a framework to organize their project, using the ACT *Student Handbook*. For example, in language arts students learn telephone skills, and in social studies they learn where to find local government telephone numbers. The second task involves keeping records of all contacts made with individuals and agencies in the community; several pages in the binder provide a structure for these records. Third, in pages titled "A Log to Show Evidence of Your Action," students record the questions they asked, what they learned, and what their next actions will be.

Section Two of the binder contains the rubric and instructions for creating a brochure and a persuasive speech. The brochure must show evidence of the community problem selected, research done, and the solution proposed by the student. It is presented to an organization when the student gives the persuasive speech. The speech is written and presented orally to an individual or local organization that the student selects. It is the public presentation of these products that inspires students to show care and pride in their work.

Section Three of the binder contains two parts. The Reflection and Poster Night Rubric provides students with the necessary information and standards to create a poster that summarizes their project. This is presented and videotaped at an evening open to parents and community members. Finally, in the Reflective Questions section, students are asked to answer questions on the process they went through, the products they created for this project, and on possibilities they would suggest to others who try a similar project.

There is one final page in the binder suggesting extra credit service; for example, a student might volunteer for a local organization that relieves hunger. Although strongly recommended, teachers believe that actual service time should be given freely. Not surprisingly, students who donate time or organize a community food drive report this as being the most satisfying activity of the project.

Assessment of students' learning is conducted throughout the service-learning project. For example, binder entries are checked frequently in class and phone calls are monitored, with redirection given as needed. Parents are also included in assessment by monitoring student progress and initialing completed sections of the binder. At the end of the project, this binder is handed in as part of the summative assessment. In addition, student products (brochure, speech, and poster) serve as important authentic assessments of their efforts.

Several challenges exist with this type of service-learning project. Because as teachers we could not anticipate all the community members students would choose to contact, we could not prearrange success for the students. We had to trust that our middle schoolers would have or develop the skills necessary to interact with a variety of different situations when contacting community members. Fortunately, the response of the community has been wonderful. Many adults have gone out of their way to spend time with students, listen to and evaluate their speeches, and push student learning beyond our initial expectations. The patience and humor extended to students has been appreciated, putting students at ease and making them feel they are a welcome and valued part of the community.

The timing of the hunger unit has also been a challenge. We had to consider the seasonal demands on local food businesses. Several student calls to grocery stores and restaurants during the winter holiday season revealed that this is not the most opportune time to request community collaboration with student projects. We have noted more community willingness to work with students when most of the research and presentations are done after the winter holidays. Also, completing their work at this time, students have become more aware of the after-holiday slump in food bank donations. This learning proved valuable this past spring when a local food bank asked our students to hold a food drive. Having completed the hunger project in late winter, the students showed a quick understanding of the problem and responded generously with time and food.

The most common challenge students report is being taken seriously when they make a phone contact. In class, students practice the tone of voice and information needed for credibility, and what polite responses to make if the student call is misinterpreted as a prank. Students rapidly improve with practice, and some report in reflective questions that the success they are most proud of is being able to conduct a business phone call. Finally, students report that completing the hunger project is challenging. Once the unit is completed, students are proud of their many accomplishments and new skills.

The overall success of the project is that it provides students with lasting educational experiences that result when there is an emotional investment by the learner. Also, the project teaches and measures social studies and language arts content standards, important in teachers' efforts to be accountable for student learning.

What successes do students report? In answers to reflective questions, students write that they are more informed, more willing to talk to strangers, and more able to stand up for the things they believe in. Furthermore, they are proud that their brochures, speeches, and posters are successful; student efforts often do result in community donations or corrective actions. Students are pleasantly surprised when they forget that this project is school work and it becomes something they care about for their community. They are also impressed that as teens, they are listened to and earn respect and trust when they speak in the community. The hunger project is rewarding educational work for students, teachers, and the community.

For more information about this service-learning project, please contact:
Diane Vliem
Moore Middle School
8455 West 88th Avenue
Arvada, Colorado 80005
phone: (303) 982-0451

Notes
1. D. Hill, J. Dunn, and P. Klein, *Global Geography System, Geographic Inquiry in Global Issues; Hunger* (Chicago, Ill.: Encyclopedia Britannica Educational Corporation, 1995).
2. Charles Degelman and Bill Hayes, *Active Citizenship Today Student Handbook* (Los Angeles, Calif.: Close Up Foundation and Alexandria, Va.: Constitutional Rights Foundation, 1995).

COMMUNITY PLANNING: PLAYGROUND REDESIGN
Deb Bradley

R. M. Marrs School, Omaha, Nebraska

SUITABLE GRADE LEVEL(S): 7-8

RELEVANT NCSS STANDARDS:

- **ⓥ INDIVIDUALS, GROUPS, AND INSTITUTIONS**
- **ⓦ POWER, AUTHORITY, AND GOVERNANCE**
- **ⓧ CIVIC IDEALS AND PRACTICES**

SOCIAL STUDIES OBJECTIVES:

1. Learn about community planning through redesigning the school's playground.

2. Work with school and community officials to develop a feasible plan.

3. Use technological tools as well as primary and secondary sources to gather and synthesize information.

PROJECT DESCRIPTION:

Each year, the seventh and eighth grade leadership teams, a group of ten students at each grade level who are selected by staff as natural positive leaders, are asked to determine a mission statement. In the fall of 1996, our principal gave us the suggestion of designing a better playground for our school. Because our school is the only K-8 school in the Omaha Public School District, it was important that our plan meet the needs of all levels of students. Our existing playground needed to be made level and had very old equipment for the elementary students. There was a small blacktop area with a basketball hoop. When we ran the mile for the Benchmark in Physical Education, we had to run across streets and on uneven sidewalks. Students practicing for track had to use a track at a neighboring high school, about one mile away. After considering all of these factors, the students decided to focus on the playground redesign as their "mission" for the school year.

That same fall, we had entered an engineering competition sponsored by the Society of Military Engineers (SAME). We quickly determined that our mission statement and competition project could be one and the same. The SAME competition had specific guidelines and deadlines that helped us to stay focused throughout the school year. Through SAME, each competing school received the help of a mentor. We were lucky to work with Captain Gary Krupa from the Army Corps of Engineers. Gary brought all the engineering expertise that we lacked.

In addition to meeting several social studies objectives set forth by the Omaha Public Schools as outlined above, we also met Omaha Instructional Process Objectives (OIPs) in the areas of language arts, math, and technology in completing this project. Most of the work on the project was done in group meetings outside of the students' regular classes, though some teachers allowed students to use class time to prepare written documentation and several helped with editing. We did have an agreement that if there was an activity in class that could not be missed, students would stay and not attend the SAME meeting. Students were also responsible for all the work that they missed. With a group of nineteen students, we were able to have several students on each working committee, which helped if any student had to miss a meeting.

Our project design had six major steps. Working together as a group to write a project statement was step one. Using the guidelines provided by SAME, step two involved identifying necessary tasks and determining committees. The tasks assigned to committees included choosing playground equipment, writing a narrative, drawing a plan to scale, making a model, taking photographs, developing cost estimates, developing a presentation, and surveying individuals in the school and local neighborhood.

Next we needed to set up a schedule with a timeline and deadlines for various aspects of the project. Gary showed us a Gannt chart, which we decided to use to show when and how much time we spent on each part of the project.

Step four involved identifying options. We had two options for how to improve the playground: one to redesign the existing area and the other to combine two teacher parking lots and make a new playground. To facilitate the next step, making choices, we broke into two groups, each exploring one of the options. The group wanting to combine the two parking lots had a major hurdle. To combine them, we had to close a section of a public street. We soon learned that we did not want to close the street, but that we wanted to "vacate" it. We found this out by calling the city planning department. A city planner explained to us in city planning terms what we wanted to do, and we subsequently received a large envelope of legal papers. The group quickly decided that one particular student could handle reading this material and then report back to everyone else.

The group working on the option to redesign the existing playground developed a survey that was given to building-level administrators, physical education teachers, coaches, elementary teachers, and elementary classrooms. The students designed the survey to get opinions about which option they preferred and what types of equipment to install. This group also sent representatives to interview the principal, who listened to the two options and had no additional options to suggest.

The student who read the papers from the city planning department then gave a report to his group. He told them that we needed to get petitions signed, that any one property owner could stop the entire process, and that it could take years to get a street vacated. The survey results from the other group indicated that most people preferred to keep the playground where it has always been. With all of this information, we decided to drop the option of combining the parking lots. We all became focused on a plan to redesign the existing playground. To develop the solution, step six, we looked at the tasks that we listed earlier for our Gannt chart. Each of these tasks was assigned to a small committee of students.

Equipment committee members took the information from the survey results and looked through catalogs until they found a play system that they felt everyone would like. They shared the ground space and protective area measurements with the plan committee so the play system would fit. The cost was computed by the cost estimate committee, and the plan committee members soon became draftsmen. Using a scale, they were able to get the play system, a five-lane track, shot put area, high jump area, and long jump area in the space we had available. The students drew the plan on a contour map of the area that the city had given us. The dimensions were given to the cost estimate committee. The cost estimate committee used the *Army TM 5-803-10, Technical Manual, Planning and Design of Outdoor Sports Facilities*, and math formulas for area and volume to determine quantities of materials needed. The students also used math to figure hours of labor for the project.

The photography committee took pictures of the existing playground and of the committees doing their specific jobs. The model committee constructed a scale model of the new playground, which helped all of us to visualize what the students had in mind. The word processing committee took all of the rough drafts from the other committees and developed the written documentation required for the SAME competition. Finally, the presentation committee determined what we needed to present our project to a panel of judges for the SAME competition.

There were many social studies objectives involved with this project. The two student groups had very different ideas about how to improve the playground. Cooperation, consideration, and compromise were all used to determine which plan would be most feasible. Students readily learned how individuals, groups, and institutions affect each other. In reviewing the information about how to vacate a street, the students were amazed to find that an individual citizen could be the deciding factor in whether a project could be pursued or not. Of all the neighbors affected, it would take only one to keep the street from being vacated.

Early on in this project, students became aware that power, authority, and governance do not always fall to the same body. The realization that institutions have their own policies and guidelines that are different from those of the governing body left the students with questions such as the following: "If the joining of the teacher parking lots was what we decided and the school district owns the property, how can the city tell the school district what it can and cannot do with the property?" "How is the decision made as to the zoning of an area?" "Are the schools an important part of the city?" These are the types of inquiries that may well lead some of these students to become lifelong active citizens.

In the documentation required for the SAME competition, and also as a reflection activity, I asked the students to list lessons they learned through working on the playground redesign. Outcomes students felt were most important included working as a team, making a big job small, following a schedule, delegating the small jobs, doing "technical things," learning about the activities of an engineer, understanding the importance of preparation, preparing a survey, learning how to make a presentation, and developing communication skills. Students experienced both difficulties and successes with each of these endeavors at some point during the project.

We also spent time reflecting through group discussions at each meeting. Although we started out with the idea of having each student keep a journal on the project, the actual project activities required more of the students' time, and the idea of maintaining a journal was abandoned in lieu of discussion.

Upon completion of their playground redesign plan for the SAME competition, the students also presented their project to the principal, who seemed genuinely pleased with what they had accomplished. We gave him a copy of the written documentation and also sent one to the Omaha Public Schools Schoolhouse Planning Department. We continue to pursue the possibility of actually implementing one or more aspects of our plan; funding is a major factor in whether or not this project becomes a reality.

At the exact time that we were presenting our project to the panel of judges, an elementary student fell, hitting his face on a piece of the existing equipment. He was then taken to an emergency room for stitches. Many people felt that newer equipment would not have had the sharp corners that caused the injury. This event has helped to continue to raise everyone's awareness of the need for a new playground.

Although we did not win the overall middle school SAME award, we did win the specific category of engineering. This was far better as we had to score higher than both high schools and middle schools to achieve this. Gary, our mentor, went on to write about his experience as our mentor for "The Military Engineer," a bimonthly publication sent worldwide to members of the Society of American Military Engineers. The article, which gave insight as to how to be a mentor, also included a photo of our school team.

Our efforts to involve seventh and eighth graders in meaningful civic participation continue to grow. Our school has been selected to be a part of the Changing Faces program, which partners the corporate world with a public school. Funding available through this program will provide several improvements at our school. Undoubtedly, we will have creative student leaders at the helm, making important decisions, considering others' interests and needs, and encouraging their peers to contribute to making their school and community a better place for everyone.

For more information about this service-learning project, please contact:
Deb Bradley
Monroe Middle School
5105 Bedford Avenue
Omaha, Nebraska 68104
phone: (402) 557-4600
e-mail: dbradley@ops.org

CHAPTER 4

SERVICE-LEARNING PROJECTS FOR HIGH SCHOOL SOCIAL STUDIES

High school students stand on the threshold of becoming adult citizens of their communities. Given this impending responsibility, service-learning projects at the high school level should provide students with increased awareness of the complexity of social issues and potential solutions and opportunities to take part in the messy and unpredictable process of trying to effect change. The four stories in this chapter reveal the ups and downs of such efforts, as well as the valuable lessons that students can learn even when their community actions do not appear to be successful. Dick Diamond tells how his students worked with sympathetic legislators to try to get a bill passed in the state legislature to improve the lives of homeless people in California. Marc Ferguson writes about the monumental effort that high school students exhibited in writing a history of their local community. In response to a request from students to connect school with the "real world," Barbara Wysocki describes how she developed the Social Advocacy course, thus providing students with first-hand experiences in learning about the lives of people living in poverty. Finally, Michaelean Monahan and Kathy Quesenberry detail how their government students worked in teams to research issues of concern identified by local government agencies. All of these stories show how high school students can exercise their citizenship skills and find real world applications for what they are learning in their social studies courses.

PUBLIC POLICY FOR THE HOMELESS
Dick Diamond
Arlington High School, Riverside, California

SUITABLE GRADE LEVEL(S): 10-12

RELEVANT NCSS STANDARDS:
- **Ⓥ INDIVIDUALS, GROUPS, AND INSTITUTIONS**
- **Ⓥ POWER, AUTHORITY, AND GOVERNANCE**
- **Ⓥ PRODUCTION, DISTRIBUTION, AND CONSUMPTION**
- **Ⓧ CIVIC IDEALS AND PRACTICES**

SOCIAL STUDIES OBJECTIVES:
1. Examine the making of public policy regarding homelessness.
2. Develop an understanding of the economic aspects of homelessness.
3. Research the issue of homelessness using a variety of sources including library materials, organizations serving homeless persons, and elected officials.
4. Learn how a bill becomes a law.
5. Develop an understanding of the role of social institutions in the creation and amelioration of homelessness.
6. Participate in the political process by formulating a bill and working to get the bill passed in the state legislature.

PROJECT DESCRIPTION:
With all of the bravado inherent in the soul of high school seniors who "know everything," Steve Ryan stood up alone in a group of one hundred of his peers, pointed his finger at State Assemblyman Steve Clute, and asked what he had done to help homeless people. None realized that this class was about to embark on an adventure that would focus the rest of our year in American Government on the passage of legislation for homeless people in California.

Three Arlington High School social studies teachers, with the complete support of the principal, decided in the spring of 1989 to challenge the class of 1990 to make a difference. The challenge was to give something back in the way of service to the community. Having a theme to the service was essential; students needed to see the relationship between their class and the world, and focus their energies on some goal. A theme would direct their energies to a specific goal. The teachers decided to focus attention on homeless people, and how society was or was not addressing their needs. This choice was not student driven, and although there was success in the endeavor, we learned that student "buy-in" was essential.

In addition to studying the problem in a school setting, separate from the "real world," students were to contribute upwards of twenty hours each semester working at soup kitchens, food banks, and the like in order to get firsthand knowledge of the issue of homelessness. Parent support was chilling at best; student attitudes at first could be aptly labeled as hostile.

The district supported us all the way to the Board of Education. We had listed a number of places for students to contribute their hours. With students selecting which places they wanted to work, insurance liability was the responsibility of the service site, rather than the school. County Counsel supported the district's contention regarding who had liability, and, fortunately, we haven't had a problem in nine years.

Initially, we were confronted with students' cries of "Why us? Why do we have to give up our precious time to help someone else?" To counter this resistance, we enlisted the support of two of the most popular students in the senior class—Sherry Izardi, our Miss Drill Team candidate, and Brian Young, a popular athlete. During summer school, there had been a pilot program in a sociology class, and our two recruits, both class leaders, had been part of that program. They got up in front of the entire senior class (350 strong) and in straightforward language stated what they had done during the summer. Brian summed up the summer's experience to his classmates by saying, "Hey, it's no big deal. Make some peanut butter and jelly sandwiches, help give someone a meal, and spread a little happiness." Peer pressure worked in our favor; we were on our way!

To integrate the program into the curriculum, we decided to approach the study of government and economics by examining the making of public policy regarding homelessness. Students studied policy formation at all levels of government during the fall and winter. The economic aspects would be studied in the spring, as we were not granted approval to combine economics and government into one year-long course. Students also focused on the project in their sociology class, where they learned about the role of social institutions in society.

The three classes (more than one hundred students) that seemed to be most enthusiastic decided to "get it from the horse's mouth." They invited elected officials from all levels of government to school to address policy and policy formation with respect to the problem of homelessness. Two city council members (one was a political science professor at the University of California, Riverside), the mayor, a member of the county Board of Supervisors, the U.S. congressional representative from our district, and our state assemblyman, Steve Clute, addressed the students over a six week period.

One council member stated that because he didn't hear of any homeless people in his district, he didn't believe there was a problem. The political science professor turned councilman recognized the problem but astonished the students by saying, "Nothing can be done to help the homeless in Riverside because they don't contribute to campaigns and they don't vote; hence they have no political clout." Following questions by the students, the councilman repeated his statement, elaborating on who gets what in politics. This was an extraordinary learning experience for the students!

The mayor said that she would like to help homeless persons, but if the city had an exemplary program, then all homeless people in southern California would come to Riverside. There just wasn't enough money to meet all of their needs. She also noted that homeless people "scared people away from the downtown area where many congregated"; in other words, they were bad for business.

The congressman explained the multiple federal studies that had been done and listed the dollars spent. The county supervisor lamented the problem, but felt it was not the county's place to establish programs in cities where the city government would be dealing with many of the social problems that would result from an influx of homeless persons. Thus far, the students had received a message of local government indifference.

Clute was the one elected official who said that more needed to be done. He congratulated the students on their effort to assist in private sector programs. It was then that Ryan asked, "Just what, Mr. Clute, have you done to help the homeless? I ride a bus twice a week to work in a soup kitchen." In a lecture hall packed with more than one hundred students from three classes, the silence was deafening. The students looked at Ryan, turned to Clute, and stared.

Without even blinking, Clute said, "To be honest, nothing. But I'll tell you what WE can do. If you come up with an idea for legislation to assist the homeless at the state level, I'll carry the bill for you. I challenge you to help me help the homeless." This was December and the legislature was scheduled to convene in February. Time to get busy!

Each of the three classes, under the guidance of their teachers, operated as a legislative committee. They held "hearings" for the next few weeks and inquired about the needs of homeless persons they felt should be addressed. All information was shared between committees. Library research was expanded to include city and university libraries. In these pre-Internet days, the students gained great skill in using various periodic guides covering all varieties of print media. The classes did not invite homeless people to class, though they did invite and learn from local groups who had been working with homeless people.

Two particular "bills" came forth. The students decided to meet as a "legislative body" in the lecture hall and vote on the legislation they wanted to present to the assemblyman. The first bill specified that shower facilities would be made available to homeless people at the selected high schools. Homeless people would be allowed to use those facilities at 6:00 a.m. in the morning. The school would provide the water, soap, and towels. Although there was effusive comment about "cleanliness being next to Godliness," the students came to realize that as noble as the idea might be, the legislature, let alone the community, wasn't going to "buy it." The students did want to accomplish something more than just getting a bill introduced. They wanted to realize a change in the state policy.

The other "bill" focused on the National Guard armories. California had the practice of opening up the armories to homeless people in the winter time when it was raining, or when the nighttime temperature fell below forty degrees. Homeless people were allowed to stay in the armories for the night but had to leave during the day (rain or shine). In addition, there was a local organization that had developed a program for supplying food for homeless people. It was this focus that would eventually wind up being written into two pieces of legislation–Assembly Bills 3512 and 3513 of the 1989-90 Regular California Session.

Because many homeless people were children, the students knew that the children needed to attend school and have some sort of address. Having studied aspects of homelessness including psychological factors, the students knew there was a need for the children to also have a place to call home, even if it was temporary. AB3512 allowed homeless persons to "reside" at the armory from October to June. Homeless people could stay at the armory during the week when there were no National Guard training activities.

The students also felt that it was important for adults who did not have a permanent address to have a place where they could receive mail. If the adults were looking for employment (or better employment, as many did work), they needed to have an address. Having an address for nine months of the year might afford those who could be phased back into the mainstream a better opportunity.

The classes also wanted to set up the armory as a temporary clearing center for health screening and job counseling. The students recognized that health screening for illnesses at an early stage, while costly, would be cheaper in the long run than emergency room care and hospital care for seriously ill people, and might reduce the possibility of contagion. Because Riverside County General was a teaching hospital for Loma Linda Medical School, the students felt that the county government could assist here. Included in this portion of the bill was a counseling and job service for those at the armory. In that way, there might be an additional opportunity for employment. It was this "bill" that the students sent to Assemblyman Clute.

Although understanding the formal procedure of a bill becoming a law, and to some extent, the "politics" of bill passage, the students were unprepared for the rewording of the bill from a champion who would support the idea with conditions. That champion was the State National Guard. The National Guard wanted the right to be able to have more control over real estate that it used. This included notification of the sale of property not owned by the National Guard but property that it used. The National Guard also wanted an advisory board to make recommendations regarding use of National Guard facilities by homeless persons. Thus, AB3512 was further developed from the students' original proposal.

Guard personnel trained in the medical field would do the screening recommended by the students; that was the subject of the second bill, AB 3513. With a student perspective developed only from Riverside, the students didn't realize that few other areas had General Hospitals that were teaching institutions. AB3513 would make medical screening available to people staying at the armories in all fifty-eight counties of California.

Via long distance phone calls from Sacramento (some 450 miles away), we received twice weekly updates of committee hearings, saw the bill as it was printed, and generally felt part of the process. To the students' amazement, the bill cleared both the Assembly and the State Senate by overwhelming margins. However, it was then vetoed by then Governor Deukmejian. The students found out later that there were forces at work that did not want the armories opened up throughout the state during the school year. They also learned that there was some controversy with the governor and the National Guard over the property control issue.

Through this experience, the students learned a great deal. In their writings, they mused over the complexities of writing a bill, the need to get lots of people working together, and the need to compromise and gather consensus to achieve a goal. They also realized much about who gets what in politics. Research skills were honed. Did they get the bill passed into law? No. Were the students successful? Yes. Both houses of the legislature passed their ideas in two bills on a controversial subject. The students learned how to be part of the political process. Teachers also learned a valuable lesson: that to get community and student buy in, we needed to allow all the "stakeholders" to participate in developing the issue to address. Thus, we now develop service-learning projects with students, rather than for them.

We could not have been successful in all aspects of community involvement without the school district's support. The extraordinary assistance of Assemblyman Clute, along with his staff, notably administrative assistant Toby Ewing, was also critical. Toby suggested sending letters to committee members, sent us samples, and informed the students of who was in favor and how to elicit more support. Through this service-learning project, students experienced the excitement and unpredictable nature of political involvement and public policy-making. They learned valuable skills in lobbying and advocacy, which, hopefully, they will continue to use to meet the needs of those who are marginalized in our society and to make our communities more just and equitable places for everyone.

For more information about this service-learning project, please contact:
Dick Diamond
Arlington High School
2951 Jackson Ave.
Riverside, California 92503
phone: (909) 788-7240
e-mail: ddiamond@ix.netcom.com

MARION COMMUNITY HISTORY
Marc Ferguson
Marion High School, Marion, Iowa

SUITABLE GRADE LEVEL(S): 10-12

RELEVANT NCSS STANDARDS:
- **❶ CULTURE**
- **❷ TIME, CONTINUITY, AND CHANGE**
- **❸ PEOPLE, PLACES, AND ENVIRONMENTS**
- **❹ INDIVIDUAL DEVELOPMENT AND IDENTITY**
- **❺ INDIVIDUALS, GROUPS, AND INSTITUTIONS**
- **❿ CIVIC IDEALS AND PRACTICES**

SOCIAL STUDIES OBJECTIVES:

1. Relate past and present national and world events to the students' community.

2. Understand how significant historical events (e.g., World War II, the Great Depression, the New Deal) affected the lives of individuals in the students' community.

3. Explore how social and cultural changes in recent decades have influenced the development of the students' community.

4. Research the history of the local community by interviewing community members, participating in community historical walks, and collecting information from city government and local agencies.

5. Work cooperatively with others toward a common goal.

6. Use writing and technological skills to make a significant contribution to the local community.

PROJECT DESCRIPTION:

Marion, Iowa, is a community with a rich history, dating back to the early 1800s as one of the leading communities in eastern Iowa. It served as the county seat from 1839 to 1919 because of its central location in the county as well as its importance in the development of the railroad. Despite this rich history, there was little documentation. One known source was a set of journals written by Marvin Oxley, a community historian. These journals, however, were not accessible to most people. With five volumes totaling 1,600 pages, only three copies existed, all housed at the local public library. During the 1994-95 school year, a class of twenty Marion High School students worked in teams of four to research, revise, and reformat these journals into a 559-page book. My teaching colleague, Scott Immerfall, and I guided students' completion of this project through both their social studies and language arts classes. Working in partnership with a local commercial art business, we were able to have more than 250 photographs scanned and cleaned up for the desktop publishing software used for compiling the text and importing the pictures. In the summer of 1995, the history book was published, for which the students were voted Marion Citizens of the Year, an annual award given by the local newspaper and Kiwanis Club.

A noted historian once stated, "We will know better where we are going if we first know where we have been." I feel that statement particularly applies when we are able to relate past and present events of the world and our nation to our own communities and neighborhoods. The Marion History project allowed students to better understand the events and figures of our history by relating them to events and figures of our own community. Students were better able to comprehend the hardships of early settlers, evaluate the social effects of war on the home front, examine the prosperity in America, assess the cause of the Depression and impact of the New Deal, evaluate the struggle for the extension of civil liberties, and explore the social and cultural changes of the most recent decades.

Funding for the project came from a variety of sources. French Studios, Inc., the local commercial art company, donated its time and labor, and $5,000 in grant money was awarded from US West and Farmers State Bank. The school board voted to financially support the rest of the publication costs, close to $30,000. Books were sold for $20 each, and profits covered the cost of publication.

The result of that initial undertaking went beyond the publication of the book, for it generated an excitement and a desire for a more contemporary history of the twentieth century (the Oxley journals covered only the periods 1838-1899 and 1917-1927). A different process, and one that would take more than two years to satisfactorily complete, had to be used while working on this second project. Because the students did not have a source such as the Oxley journals from which to begin, they were faced with the challenge of starting from scratch. The process began with the class selecting related topics from the decade or era of American history they were studying. They then related those topics to their Marion community, researched their topics, and wrote an article. The class split into teams of two to four students, and each team selected the topic of its choice. Then, it was the students' responsibility to locate reliable sources and go out into the community to find information concerning their specific article. The students then gathered information in their teams by writing questions, conducting interviews, reading historical documents, and so on. Finally, as soon as enough information was gathered about one topic, the students compiled all of the information and created an article on desktop publishing for the book. The last piece of the puzzle was locating or taking photographs to illustrate and enhance the articles.

During the 1996-97 and 1997-98 school years, students took suggestions from community readers of the first draft and went about improving and revising the draft from the previous year. Students from both years located additional photographs and researched and wrote additional historical text. The final edition was 209 pages in length with a total of 216 photographs. In February of 1998, a presentation was made to school board members, who again agreed to provide the funds necessary for publication. We also obtained grant funds of $4,000; the school board funded the difference in the $10,000 printing cost (this was a smaller book, with fewer copies).

This project allowed the students the opportunity to interact with a large number of community citizens, businesses, and additional resources in ways that traditional classes usually don't. Students were involved in every step of the decision-making process and were in day-to-day contact with people in the community. This interaction benefited both the students and the community citizens. Local businesses supported the project by allowing students to use sophisticated technology to help prepare the books for publication. Additional community resources used in the research process were public, private, and Masonic libraries; historical museums; the local cemetery; local historical sites; county and city government facilities (i.e., City Hall and Chamber of Commerce); local businesses; local media (i.e., newsletters, newspapers, radio, and television); senior centers and nursing homes; and, of course, community citizens with knowledge of students' research topics.

The students have been stakeholders in determining their own progress and assessing the project, and as a result have begun to view themselves as contributing members of the Marion community. Students were involved in ongoing reflection and assessment activities, including team building and goal setting, conferences with their community mentors or teachers, journal writing, and even videotaping responses to questions in order to aid students' presentations to audiences or the media. This project was a monumental task for the students, considering the small amount of documented information available to them. The students were able to complete this book and provide memories and testimony of the events and people from the rich history that has shaped Marion into the outstanding city it is today.

As a result of the success of this project, it has been expanded each year to include more students. Marion history has been more fully integrated into the social studies curriculum, at both the elementary and secondary level, using books that were developed by the Marion students as supplemental resources. Recent activities related to community history included historical walks and presentations given by high school students to all fourth grade students in the district. Students from a commercial art class researched and created pieces with historical scenes and buildings that are mounted on a wall at the high school. When gravestones were replaced for Civil War soldiers in the local cemetery, the American Legion recruited Marion students to research and write biographical sketches of the soldiers. Some of those students, as well as others, were readers at an Armed Forces Community Celebration held at the local cemetery, and elementary and secondary instrumental and vocal students provided music relevant to the time period.

The Marion History project is only one of many service-learning experiences reaching into the community and involving administration, staff, and students throughout the district. Projects such as this could not occur without the strong support of administrators, who allowed students the opportunity to leave campus to conduct field research. Our administrators, along with the parents who gave written permission, had enough faith in the staff and students involved to give them the responsibility that goes with such an undertaking.

Certainly one of the benefits of including a service element in the social studies curriculum is that it will benefit the community, but equally important is the benefit for the student, the educational opportunity to interact with community citizens and actively participate in community affairs. Students gain a deeper appreciation for their community, for its past, and for the people who presently live in it. They begin to see themselves as a resource to their community and learn the valuable lesson of becoming a contributing citizen. This is a lesson educators hope to instill in young people, so that when they are adults, they will take the reins as civic leaders in their own communities. The Marion History project allowed us the opportunity to do just that. We learned about the people and the institutions of our community by interacting with them, and by learning about those closest to home, we learned about other people in our nation and throughout the world.

For more information about this service-learning project, please contact:
Marc Ferguson
Marion High School
675 S. 15th Street
Marion, Iowa 52302
phone: (319) 377-9891
e-mail: mferguson@marion.k12.ia.us
To purchase the two-book Marion History set, please send $20,
which includes postage and handling, to Marc Ferguson.

SOCIAL ADVOCACY: HISTORY, THEORY, AND PRACTICE
Barbara L. Wysocki
University Laboratory High School, Urbana, Illinois

SUITABLE GRADE LEVEL(S): 11-12

RELEVANT NCSS STANDARDS:
- **❶ CULTURE**
- **❷ TIME, CONTINUITY, AND CHANGE**
- **❹ INDIVIDUAL DEVELOPMENT AND IDENTITY**
- **❺ INDIVIDUALS, GROUPS, AND INSTITUTIONS**
- **❻ POWER, AUTHORITY, AND GOVERNANCE**
- **❽ SCIENCE, TECHNOLOGY, AND SOCIETY**
- **❿ CIVIC IDEALS AND PRACTICES**

SOCIAL STUDIES OBJECTIVES:
1. Learn about selected social problems, their historical development, and solutions that have been attempted.
2. Examine the fundamental questions that underlie political philosophies.
3. Read literary texts (fiction/nonfiction) related to social issues.
4. Critically analyze the role of popular culture in American society.
5. Develop knowledge about people and organizations addressing social needs in the local community.
6. Think and act creatively as citizens in a democratic society.
7. Reflect on and clarify one's values in relation to social issues in U.S. society.
8. Exchange ideas and opinions with others on relevant social issues.

PROJECT DESCRIPTION:
In response to student concerns that they were leaving high school knowing a lot about math and science but very little about the "real world," Audrey Wells, an English instructor, and I developed the Social Advocacy course in the mid-1980s. Students asked for a course that would put them in touch with their local community, with people facing the daily struggles of living as single working mothers, homeless persons, or persons unable to read or write. Social Advocacy would become a link between the sheltered environment of the school and the life of the community.

We designed the class to focus on the community's social problems by dealing with a series of core questions such as, What is society? What is a healthy society? Why do we have social problems? Who is affected by these problems? How do you define yourself? How has your identity been shaped by your society? Do you affect the shape of society? Who or what creates culture? Can culture be changed? What is the relationship between popular culture and social problems? How does television affect society? What is necessary to solve or remedy a social problem? What are the roles of individual citizens/ the private sector/ government (local, state, national) in remedying social problems?

Students taking Social Advocacy have either had or are currently in a U.S. History course. Therefore, this elective course can focus in on select aspects of cultural development over time, for example, the concept of welfare from 1930-90; the role of reformers as exemplified by individual, group, and institutional efforts in effecting change (e.g., Jane Addams, the Catholic Worker Movement, churches); and the changing role of government (local, state, federal) in addressing social issues.

One of the opening exercises in Social Advocacy is a group activity in which students use Tinker Toys to reproduce their image of society. Their designs very clearly bring out their ideas of who or what controls society, what the various components are, and what roles are played by ordinary people. We then invite our mayor, the township supervisor, and local advocacy groups to class to share their perspectives on social service expenditures as part of the city budget and other related community issues.

Because of its English/history roots, Social Advocacy has deep connections in both areas. The reading assignments, for example, are both fiction and nonfiction, enabling students to compare their experience of people with those portrayed in literature. Students write a short story that encourages them to get "into another person's skin" and experience a day from that vantage point. Students also use nonfiction literature to examine more closely the personal and social implications of an issue such as teenage parenting or foster care.

Because the focus of this course is on American society and its social problems, we acquaint students with social theories about who and what shape contemporary culture. Through Michael Harrington's book *The Other America*, students come to know about the "culture of poverty," the concept whereby Harrington suggests that people living in poverty come to develop a set of behaviors that can only be traced to their economic status.[1]

To make this concept more real, students do a "Living Poor" exercise in which they are given a hypothetical situation and income level. Their task is to establish a budget, identifying fixed costs and discretionary money. With their allocation for food and a week's worth of menus in hand, students then go to a local grocery story to "purchase" the food items. At some point, a crisis is imposed in the exercise (e.g., an accident, a job lay off, changes in welfare) that forces them to adjust their budgets and underscores the precarious nature of the lives of those who are poor.

Social Advocacy also provides a unit on the media and its influence on American society and culture. We examine the sitcom from the fifties to the nineties, asking if the portrayal of families, for example, is mirroring American life or communicating an ideal of family values. We examine advertising and its use of female images to examine what connections there may be to women who are abused or economically powerless. Through reading John Howard Griffin's *Black Like Me*, students can better assess the role of institutional racism in the 1950s and compare it to the contemporary scene.[2]

Our community hosts a few mass production operations that pay low wages and offer no benefits. A tour of these facilities enables the students to understand the concept of "the working poor," the high turnover in employees, and the effects of downsizing. Students also realize that electronic technology facilitates communication between social agencies, a volunteer on-line site that connects people to volunteer opportunities, and demands a certain level of education to make people employable.

In addition to its social problems focus, Social Advocacy is a course in self-discovery. Students are encouraged to examine their personal attitudes, prejudices, and values regarding society and to see themselves in relationship to the whole. One activity that reinforces these objectives is the completion of a personal sociological portrait, using an anthropological model. Students treat themselves as subjects by objectively describing a common occurrence in the family (e.g., mealtime, morning routine) in a paper. Students provide careful details of the physical setting, the role of each family member, and the interactions that take place. After painting a picture of the scene, students analyze the data as a sociologist might: What inferences can be made about income, political affiliation, and religious and educational background? What evidence is there about age, race, and gender? We model this exercise by videotaping living rooms of our friends (but unknown to the students) and ask students to examine the evidences of race, class, and ethnicity as a way to determine information about the occupants. As the students share their portraits, they begin to see patterns and divergences from which they can determine what assumptions can or cannot be made about people. Through the sociological portrait, students come to a realization of who they are or, at least, how they are defined by the broader society (e.g., advertisers, television, politicians). They also begin to realize and articulate their perspectives on the causes and effects of social problems, as well as their solutions.

Although all of these activities provide students with valuable learning experiences, they receive firsthand knowledge of social issues through the people who are dealing with them. To set up the service aspect of the course, we first visited our local United Way staff, who were very helpful in recommending social service agencies that were possible matches with our hopes for the class. We then visited those agencies, shared our vision of the course with them, and invited them to collaborate with us in this endeavor. They agreed to take our students as volunteers; the students would receive information and insights about illiteracy, homelessness, aging, and the like from the experience. This placement plus readings, guest speakers, field trips, and class discussions would assist students in evaluating, reflecting, and forming an opinion on the social issues we studied.

By volunteering in homeless shelters, literacy centers, health care facilities, and the like, students have an opportunity to connect names and faces with particular social issues. Students generally volunteer two to four hours a week outside of the school day. Although some go in the evenings, most complete their volunteer work on the weekends. By spending hours every week at their volunteer assignment, students begin to notice the frequency with which people use the facility, the interactions between the clients or residents, the philosophy of the site, and a number of other subtleties.

Opportunities to reflect on their service experiences are provided frequently in our class meetings. Each week, time is devoted to sharing and reflecting on students' most recent volunteer experiences. Sometimes the sharing is done in a large group, sometimes just among the students who are at the same site. Students are expected to keep a journal in which they record thoughts, impressions, and insights that reveal much about their personal journey. Journals are read by the teachers as a way to continue communication on an individual basis, to assess students' learning, and to challenge their thinking. Reflection also takes other forms. Sometimes a simple drawing conveys students' satisfaction or frustrations; role playing in class can also reveal how things are going or indicate unease in the volunteer situation.

Community involvement occurs on several levels. The placement of students in social service agencies requires that the site coordinator become a teacher and active mentor to the students in addition to being a supervisor, providing direction for the students and their work. Community resources also provide a wealth of field trip experiences and guest speakers in the classroom. The ideal combination occurs when an agency head comes to class and shares the history and philosophical background of the agency, and then we visit the site, returning to class for discussion and quiet reflection. Most important, students are relating to, and sometimes befriending, people from outside their circle and seeing social problems in human as well as academic terms.

Over the thirteen years of this course, our students have earned a reputation for being serious, reliable, and humane workers. One of the benefits of our reputation has been agencies calling with requests for help with one-time special projects. Many times there are annual fund-raising projects that require extra personnel. Honoring these requests is an excellent way to explore new possibilities, forge new relationships, involve students in the school's lower grade levels, and broaden the students' awareness of community services and their ability to serve.

Evaluation is an important component of the Social Advocacy course.[3] We use four methods to evaluate students. First, we grade their participation in class. We expect students to be actively engaged in discussions, contributing to the information and insights of their peers, and responding to the stimulation offered by guest speakers, field trips, and readings. Second, we evaluate their journals. We expect entries after each volunteer experience, at assigned times in class, and as a thoughtful instrument for personal growth and exploration. Third, we assess the students' volunteer experiences. We visit the site while they are working, note their interactions with staff and clients, and discuss their progress with the supervisor. Finally, we grade the written assignments given throughout the year. Because these are written essays, traditional standards are used.

Students also have continual opportunities to evaluate the course. They offer feedback and suggestions for speakers, topics, and field experiences. At the conclusion of the course, students do a formal evaluation of the content, methodology, and instruction. Over the years, we have incorporated a number of student suggestions and ideas, tailoring the course to the needs of the students.

We look upon the Social Advocacy course as an initiation—an approach to responsible citizenship by raising life-long questions rather than a course that comes to a conclusion as the semester closes. Therefore, the traditional final exam never seemed to be an appropriate way to end the class. Instead, we hold a symposium at which students present poster projects that reflect their dreams about solutions to social problems they've learned about during the class. Parents, agency heads, and classmates are invited to hear their presentations and comment on the ideas. Following the presentations, students are awarded certificates of appreciation; conversation usually continues over refreshments.

This elective class, over its thirteen year history, has seemed to attract students who are open to and/or inclined toward this teaching methodology and subject matter. The students who take the class find it rewarding and affirming, as suggested by their course evaluations at the end of each year. Over the long term, students report continuing some kind of volunteer work, especially while they are in college. Some students report having refocused their college major, moving away from pure research in medicine, for example, toward something more people-oriented or something that brings them closer to individuals with real needs.

The core questions posed by Social Advocacy are life-long questions that every citizen in a democracy should be asking all the time. By introducing students to volunteering, by supporting and affirming them, and by continuing to volunteer ourselves, we are communicating that civic involvement should be an integral aspect of everyone's life.

For more information about this service-learning project, please contact:
Barbara L. Wysocki
University Laboratory High School
1212 W. Springfield Avenue
Urbana, IL 61801
phone: (217) 333-2870
e-mail: bwysocki@uni.uiuc.edu

Notes
1. Michael Harrington, *The Other America* (New York: Penguin Books, 1984).
2. John Howard Griffin, *Black Like Me* (New York: Penguin Books, 1960).
3. For more details about the process of evaluation, see Barbara L. Wysocki, "Evaluating Students in a Course on Social Advocacy," *Social Education* 63, no. 6 (October 1999): 346-350.

GOVERNMENT SERVICE-LEARNING
Michaelean Monahan
James Wood High School, Winchester, Virginia
Kathy Quesenberry Fout
Sherando High School, Stephens City, Virginia

SUITABLE GRADE LEVEL(S): 11-12

RELEVANT NCSS STANDARDS:

- **Ⓥ INDIVIDUALS, GROUPS, AND INSTITUTIONS**
- **Ⓥ POWER, AUTHORITY, AND GOVERNANCE**
- **Ⓥ PRODUCTION, DISTRIBUTION, AND CONSUMPTION**
- **Ⓧ CIVIC IDEAS AND PRACTICES**

SOCIAL STUDIES OBJECTIVES:

1. Identify various political and economic systems and the political values that support these systems.

2. Explain the basic principles underlying the American Constitution and identify the events leading to and the compromises made at the Constitutional Convention.

3. Describe the two levels of government and identify the powers of each level.

4. Describe the structure and function of the three branches of the national government as well as the checks and balances that exist among the branches.

5. Identify the constitutional protections that exist in the Bill of Rights and Fourteenth Amendment and recognize the role of the Supreme Court in defining these liberties.

6. Identify the structure of state and local governments and analyze contemporary problems facing these institutions.

7. Recognize the role of citizen in one's local community.

8. Apply various research skills to problem solve particular issues relating to community needs.

9. Develop the ability to participate in the democratic process at the community level.

10. Identify how the components of federal, state, and local governments interact at the community level and how an average citizen can have an impact on that interaction.

PROJECT DESCRIPTION:

The Government 12 Service-Learning class in Frederick County, Virginia, is an attempt to transform twelfth grade students in U.S. Government classes from passive recipients to active participants in the teaching and learning process, while emphasizing the development of citizenship skills. The students use the local community as an extended learning laboratory in which they are given the opportunity to apply the knowledge and skills they have acquired in their government class to develop possible solutions to community problems or issues that are affecting the Winchester/Frederick County area. Students select their service learning projects based on actual problems and issues that have been identified by local governmental agencies.

The Government 12 Service-Learning class is one section of a state-required U.S. Government class. Students are selected for this class via an application process based on grades, attendance, and references; parental permission is also required. The principals, directors of guidance, and the service-learning teachers and coordinators work together to select the students.

During the first semester of the Government 12 Service-Learning class, students complete all the course work for the Government 12 curriculum as required by the Virginia Board of Education. During the second semester, students spend approximately half of their class time in various local governmental agency placements working on their service learning projects, which they select based on their individual interests. Students work in groups of three in agencies such as the County Treasurer, Commissioner of Revenue, County Planning, Public Works, Health Department, Commonwealth Attorney, Clerk of the Court, and Fire and Rescue. Students are required to provide their own transportation to and from their placements. They are expected to sign in and out when leaving their schools, and are also required to sign in and out of their agency placement and to return to their schools at the appropriate time. These expectations strengthen the students' sense of accountability and responsibility.

An essential component of the class is to ensure that the service-learning projects designed by the agencies for the students to complete not only have substantive value for the agencies but also a serious instructional component for the students relative to their knowledge of local government. We find it imperative to work closely with the community partners/agencies in designing the specific projects. Some of the service-learning projects that students have completed include (1) a study of the feasibility of introducing a local income tax; (2) a cost-benefit analysis of using the local detoxification center to deal with public inebriates in more productive community service versus incarceration in the local jail; (3) the feasibility of countywide curbside trash pick-up versus the standard dump sites; (4) the availability of low-income housing in the county in the future; (5) a study to determine the effectiveness of the local health department's immunization program; and (6) the impact of the National Voter Registration Act on the local registrar's office and voter turnout.

The Government 12 Service Learning project has the full cooperation of the school board, the county administrator, and the local Board of Supervisors in the placement of students in local governmental agencies during the school day. Not all agencies, however, have the flexibility or staff to give the students the same amount of guidance and instruction.

Because the students are assigned to the local governmental agencies in groups of three, they quickly have to develop various group dynamic skills in addition to learning about division of labor, time management, and collaborative work skills. Because some groups have more guidance than others from their agency supervisors, the importance of selecting the proper placements becomes apparent.

On days when students are not in the community at their placements, they return to the classroom and spend time sharing their service-learning experiences with each other. They critique each other's service-learning projects and attempt to solve some of the problems they encounter in accessing information for their projects. Readings on the concepts of democracy, civic participation, and citizenship are assigned for in-class days. Students frequently relate these readings to their service-learning experiences in the community, which helps to make the concepts and ideas taught in class far less abstract and much more real for the students.

While students are involved in various community placements during the second semester, their work is evaluated through the use of daily logs, periodic project updates, and deadlines. Students produce a final written project, which provides for the reinforcement of their research and writing skills. The students present their projects at a countywide evening forum attended by members of the local government, county agencies, school officials, parents, and members of the general public. Each project is presented in detail using technology media, such as Power Point. The results are enthusiastically received by the community audience, and the students express pride in what they have accomplished.

The projects have been valuable to the respective local government agencies as some of the students' recommendations are already being seriously considered by the county officials for implementation. Curbside trash pickup will likely become a reality. The immunization program operated by the local health department will undergo some changes. Inmates at the regional jail will probably be given the opportunity to participate in a work release program in the near future.

The Government 12 Service-Learning students experience a genuine sense of personal accomplishment for having made a meaningful contribution to their community. Students have begun to develop a different attitude about their roles as citizens in the community, as they see their work as valuable to their respective agencies and begin to view the work of their agencies as something very valuable to the community. They have also expressed the desire to be part of positive solutions rather then possibly being viewed by their community as part of a problem. This insight is not something that can be taught in a traditional government classroom setting.

Parental support has been outstanding. Parents have commented that their sons and daughters are initiating conversations at the dinner table about local governmental issues and are talking about their service-learning projects. Others have shared that these young people are more frequently reading local newspapers to learn about county governmental issues. The students' renewed interests have, in some cases, prompted their parents to become more informed about local issues.

At the conclusion of the Government 12 Service-Learning class, students talk about the importance of citizens becoming more informed and involved in their community in a positive manner rather than placing unreasonable demands on local government agencies.

Their commitment continues even after graduation, as some students work with their agencies during the summer in presenting their project findings to other local governments in the region. The students' confidence, oral communications, presentation skills, and pride have increased with each opportunity to share their service-learning projects with other audiences. Many of the students now say they plan to register, vote, and become involved in their community because they believe they can make a difference.

Although the Government 12 Service-Learning project has been successful in Frederick County, it should serve not as a blueprint, but rather as an example that can be modified in other school districts and communities. The proximity of an adequate number of local governmental agencies staffed by individuals willing to work with students may be a problem in some rural areas. Commitment and flexibility on the part of the school district is essential, as well as community commitment and cooperation.

Teachers who aspire to create a program similar to our Government 12 Service-Learning class must be prepared to assume much additional work that can become quite time consuming. Funding for such a labor-intensive program can also be a major obstacle because today many school districts have serious budgetary constraints. Our local project was fortunate to receive a two-year grant to pay for the additional expenses from the national Surdna Foundation through its effective citizenry initiative.

As a result of the Frederick County Government 12 Service-Learning project, our beliefs have been affirmed that the experiences students gain by working hand-in-hand with community partners on meaningful projects is a lesson in citizenship that will not be forgotten once students have graduated. As one service-learning student observed, "People need to wake up and get involved, and they won't be so bored with the government because there is so much to learn and so much to do."

For more information about this service-learning project, please contact:

Michaelean Monahan	*Kathy Quesenberry Fout*
James Wood High School	*Sherando High School*
161 Apple Pie Ridge Road	*185 South Warrior Drive*
Winchester, VA 22603	*Stephens City, VA 22655*
phone: (540) 667-5226	*phone: (540) 869-0060*

CHAPTER 5

SERVICE-LEARNING IN SOCIAL STUDIES TEACHER EDUCATION

Joan Rose

Indiana University Southeast, New Albany, Indiana

If the concept of service-learning is to reach its potential in K-12 education, both preservice and in-service teachers need to know how to design appropriate curriculum and to implement sound service-learning projects. In this chapter, I discuss strategies for including service-learning in social studies teacher education based on my teaching experience at Indiana University Southeast in an undergraduate social studies methods course and related field experience, as well as in a graduate service-learning workshop.

My undergraduate students and I maintain a close working partnership with public school colleagues at S. Ellen Jones Elementary in New Albany, Indiana, where grant funds from the Indiana Department of Education (via the Corporation for National Service) have supported a schoolwide service-learning program for five years. The service-learning activities in the teacher education program at Indiana University Southeast have been supported through joint funding from Indiana Campus Compact and the Indiana Department of Education under the Embedding Service-learning into Teacher Education (ESTE) Program. In addition, my work in service-learning as an individual faculty member has been supported during the 1996-97 academic year through the Indiana Campus Compact Learn and Serve Faculty Fellows Program.

SERVICE-LEARNING PROVIDES A NATURAL CONTEXT FOR BUILDING EXPERTISE

Service-learning provides a natural context in which future teachers can expand their knowledge about teaching and learning in circumstances that are rich and real. Our job, as program-based teacher educators, is to help preservice teachers lay the foundation for continued development of expertise in teaching. Building expertise involves much more than knowing facts. It is based on a deep knowledge of the challenges associated with teaching and learning in today's schools. Planning appropriate experiences that truly help preservice teachers discover that deep knowledge is our challenge.

Caine and Caine suggest that all learners should be immersed in activities that are personally meaningful and challenging and, further, that learners must be given the opportunity to process these experiences.[1] The term "orchestrated immersion" is used to describe teaching that takes information off the page and the blackboard and brings it to life in the minds of students. When we involve preservice teachers along with K-12 students in compelling experiences, such as helping elderly persons, interacting with persons with disabilities, and investigating social inequities, we are asking them to develop and employ complex thinking skills. By immersing preservice teachers in the pedagogy of service-learning, we afford them the opportunity to become designers of experiences for children that are meaningful and effective and that support a host of civic and social goals present in a democratic society.

SERVICE-LEARNING HELPS TO DEVELOP SKILLS AND DISPOSITIONS WE VALUE

Service-learning builds awareness of what it means to live lives of connection in caring communities. Authentic learning naturally flows when both information and personal involvement are present. The research on service-learning shows that it is a positive contributor to the development of outcomes we have always desired for future teachers, namely, that they feel positive about themselves and teaching, that they become self-aware and able to advocate for all children, that they are able to help children develop complex thinking and problem solving skills, and that they feel empowered to "make a difference" in their world through facilitating the learning of children.[2] Service-learning supports the preparation of teachers to work within our multicultural society and engage in reforms aimed at authentic learning.[3] Research has documented that service-learning has positive effects on preservice teachers' personal development, career awareness, and self-efficacy regarding their ability to help solve the problems of society.[4]

Teacher educators have identified several rationales for including service-learning in a teacher education program. These include (1) to give preservice teachers practice in designing reflection activities for students,[5] (2) to help preservice teachers develop a student-centered approach to teaching,[6] and (3) to extend their visions of the teaching role to encompass counselor, community liaison, and moral leader.[7]

SERVICE-LEARNING IS A TOOL TO ORGANIZE REQUIRED CURRICULA

Instructional units based on service-learning fit easily into local and state curricular guidelines and many of the conceptual models and frameworks currently in use by K-12 schools. As a teaching strategy, service-learning is particularly well-suited to the goals and objectives of social studies teacher education. The National Council for the Social Studies' standards themes are based on the traditional social science disciplines—building on the interconnectedness of these disciplines and providing structure for understanding society and citizenship goals.[8] Service-learning projects often involve issues of civic participation, such as balancing the rights and responsibilities of individuals and groups, negotiating the process of changing a procedure or law, or simply obtaining permission to complete a public improvement project. Links between service-learning and the performance expectations associated with NCSS Standards are plentiful and easy to access, as demonstrated by the K-12 project descriptions in this bulletin.

SERVICE-LEARNING PRESENTS IMPORTANT CHALLENGES

Although service-learning as a methodology presents great opportunities for teachers and students, we have also learned through recent research and experience that service-learning programs in both K-12 schools and teacher education programs present demands of training, time, financial resources, and administrative support that must be considered.[9] In view of this basic concern, it is necessary for the teacher educator to make the role of teacher-as-facilitator explicit while providing the necessary emotional and practical support to help the preservice teacher respond positively to these challenges. For example, teacher educators can assist preservice teachers in learning about simple ways to acquire funding (e.g., bake sales, small grants, admission to special school events) and volunteer support (e.g., parents, community members, school staff) for school-based service-learning projects.

One significant challenge in undergraduate teacher education is overcoming traditional views of teaching and learning and changing the dynamics of the classroom. Wade observed that "most students enter teacher education programs with largely traditional views that they have acquired over a dozen years of schooling. . . . Challenging belief structures created early in life remains a decidedly difficult task."[10] This is particularly important in regard to preparing teachers to teach diverse populations. Several teacher educators have noted the difficulties in fostering preservice teachers' abilities and willingness to question cultural norms about diversity and poverty[11] or to develop a stronger commitment to social justice.[12] Many have noted, however, that service-learning is an effective strategy for enhancing preservice teachers' awareness and acceptance of diverse youth.[13]

It is also important to thoroughly immerse the preservice or in-service teacher in a leadership role when possible. In their study of the student teaching experience, Wade and Yarborough found that student teachers who were centrally involved in the planning and implementation of a service-learning project felt more empowered and had more positive outcomes.[14] Student evaluations from my methods course also verify that preservice teachers who feel they are the primary leaders in a service-learning project rate the experience more positively. Furthermore, some of the most positive comments on student evaluations have come when the preservice teacher had more knowledge and understanding of the service-learning process than the cooperating teacher.

The challenges of time, financial resources, and administrative support are more concrete and can be addressed through building linkages and relationships within and between universities, schools, and communities. In the descriptions that follow, I explain how I worked with these challenges in my methods courses and their related field experience.

SERVICE-LEARNING IN ELEMENTARY SOCIAL STUDIES METHODS

Five goals for the undergraduate social studies methods course at Indiana University Southeast (IUS) include the following: (1) to develop positive attitudes and perceptions about the teaching of social studies; (2) to relate principles and theories from the course to actual practice in classrooms and schools; (3) to plan and manage appropriate lessons and units for social studies instruction; (4) to use the concept of service-learning as a social studies strategy; and (5) to understand and apply the National Council for Social Studies (NCSS) Standards as a framework for lesson and unit development, program evaluation, and student assessment. Additional goals for the related field experience include the following: (1) to experience the role of teacher as facilitator and coach of the learning process and (2) to contribute to the learning experiences of children.

There are some requirements I think of as "general requirements" for the methods course, which include reflecting on journal articles, comparing Internet sites, attending instructor conferences, comparing textbooks, creating a group unit based on a textbook with a service-learning project, making a group presentation that includes ideas for service-learning projects related to specific social studies disciplines, and designing a resource unit that may be related to the field experience service-learning project or may include an entirely new project idea. Class sessions for the undergraduate social studies methods course provide background information, curriculum design and assessment skills, processing activities, and reflection opportunities.

The field experience, consisting of an orientation, class observations, a planning session with the cooperating teacher, five lessons, and a celebration (frequently schoolwide), provide opportunities to put theory into practice with support from a classroom teacher in a school setting. Lessons implemented in the field experience are directly related to the key elements of service-learning (e.g., assessment of needs and resources, preparation, decision making, reflection) and must be specifically tied to NCSS themes and performance expectations.

SUPPLEMENTARY MATERIALS AND STRATEGIES
BUILD BACKGROUND KNOWLEDGE

Students' successful use of service-learning as pedagogy in their field experiences requires supplementing the regular social studies methods text with readings, videos, testimonials, guest speakers, and other strategies. At the beginning of the semester, I provide a number of journal citations with choices for required readings via my website, which contains an electronic version of my course syllabus with links to related resources. These citations for appropriate readings are arranged into four categories (General Social Studies, Service-Learning, Performance Assessment, and Portfolio Assessment) with several choices in each category. The structured readings are spaced throughout the semester and help to establish the group's knowledge base about social studies and service-learning connections and continually invite the reader to consider theory/practice issues. For example, the reflection papers associated with these readings include key ideas, questions, connections to social studies, application ideas, and insights. From semester to semester, I have noted the articles that seem to yield the richest reflections and weeded the selections accordingly.

Although we have an excellent selection of children's literature at IUS, I have found that my students need explicit help in selecting appropriate literature to assist in the development of a service-learning theme. I have recently collaborated with my literacy college to identify and maintain appropriate text sets that support service-learning topics, such as the situation of elderly persons, endangered animals, and homelessness. These text sets may include poems, essays, children's literature, and illustrations. Although many of these items are already in our collection, I believe the convenience and organization of the text sets into these categories will assist the students in identifying high-quality literature that will support content, feelings, and values associated with issues and social concerns that relate to service-learning projects occurring during the semester.

SERVICE-LEARNING IS REAL SOCIAL STUDIES

Preservice teachers expect a social studies methods course to "prepare me to teach social studies." Accordingly, I find it helps to make the connection between service-learning and the traditional social studies disciplines (e.g., history, geography, economics) very clear. I do this at every opportunity possible, through class discussion, reflection activities, and specific assignments. For instance, one assignment requires students in the class to break into groups for a study of each of the ten NCSS themes (e.g., Culture; Time, Continuity, and Change; People, Places, and Environments) and associated performance expectations. A part of this assignment asks that students create a class presentation and handout that illustrate typical content, methods, and resources associated with the assigned theme. Students must also suggest service-learning projects that could assist K-12 students in meeting appropriate performance expectations. Preservice teachers present lesson plans, materials, Internet sources, and journal readings as illustrations for the connections they have made. This is often an eye-opening experience for students who then begin to see the potential for service-learning to enhance social studies education.

Another assignment aimed at creating strong connections between the social studies curriculum and service-learning requires teams of students to discover how a service-learning project can evolve from the content of a traditional textbook chapter. In small groups, students brainstorm and develop an outline of an instructional unit based on the chapter. A portion of this assignment is devoted to considering each of the key elements of service-learning and developing a description of how that element could be implemented in a suggested project. A final summary for the assignment asks the students to explain how service and learning are connected in the group unit plan. As students complete this assignment, they begin to see that service ideas can easily flow out of textbook material and other required curricula.

A major assignment at the end of the course brings these curriculum design experiences and the service-learning field experience together in a final resource unit in which, again, students are asked to show the specific curricular connections and reflect on strengths and weaknesses of their design as it relates to balancing the NCSS themes and performance expectations, thinking skills, kinds of intelligences, local and state curriculum proficiencies, service-learning elements, kinds of class groupings, and subject matter connections.

TAKING A RISK—GETTING BACK INTO THE CLASSROOM

A prerequisite to establishing a quality field experience is establishing a quality relationship with your school partners and their respective community agencies. In my research on school-community partnerships, I observed how important it is for key individuals in the partnership to have credibility both at the university and in the school.[15] Professors are often viewed as individuals who have theoretical knowledge but lack practical experience. It is important for school partners to see university personnel as having firsthand knowledge about the exigencies and pace of the public school environment. In order to strengthen my credibility with my school partners and preservice teachers, I have sought opportunities to renew my classroom skills within the public school environment. Twice in the past five years I have intentionally taken the time at the end of spring semester to personally conduct short-term (six weeks) exploratory service-learning courses in a middle school setting. One was structured around my special interest of quilting and the other around the social problem of homelessness. Each experience exposed me to middle school students and allowed me to model service-learning practices within a school. They have also served as a vivid reminder to me of the practical considerations that accompany the idealism of "making the world a better place." My theoretical understandings have been tempered with the very real experience of "what works" in today's classroom. Recalling these experiences helps me empathize with my students and helps promote my credibility in public school practicum settings. I highly recommend them to anyone wishing to understand and remain "in touch" with the everyday life of teachers and students in schools.

BUILD A STRUCTURE THAT SUPPORTS A SUCCESSFUL PRESERVICE EXPERIENCE

Another important consideration in planning a quality field experience is establishing an organized method of doing business. At S. Ellen Jones Elementary, where I have been taking my students for five years, we asked for a budget line in the grant funds mentioned earlier to hire a service-learning coordinator. This individual takes care of communication between school and university (e.g., arranges meetings), helps plan receptions and celebrations, arranges bus transportation for field trips, helps document service activities, and assists cooperating and preservice teachers in obtaining necessary supplies for projects. In addition, we have formed a small informal planning group that meets before school each semester two or three times to establish a schedule of events for the semester, plan the orientation and the celebration, and discuss other logistical concerns. This group consists of myself, the principal, the service-learning coordinator, a primary and an intermediate teacher, and one or two preservice teachers. After several semesters of working together, group members form friendships and bonds that make planning and problem solving easier. It is not always the case that an entire school will become involved in the service-learning initiatives, yet a high-quality collaboration with support from both the public school and the university is likely to encourage many teachers to participate.

PROVIDE A WELL-ORCHESTRATED ORIENTATION TO THE FIELD EXPERIENCE

I find that my students are always concerned about how they will be received in the school setting. In addition, they are sometimes anxious about extending themselves beyond the classroom into the community. One of the most helpful strategies I have found to ease these concerns is a well-planned orientation day aimed at creating a hospitable environment in the school that promotes feelings of safety and trust. This orientation is collaboratively planned by the small group mentioned above. Signs of professional "specialness" and respect are given to preservice teachers in the form of name tags and folders of information. A continental breakfast is provided with time to chat and welcome each preservice teacher to the school.

A typical orientation lasts from 8:30 a.m. until the end of the school day, with an hour for "lunch on your own." In the morning, preservice teachers are welcomed by the principal, who communicates the seriousness with which she/he and the staff approach service-learning and what the activities of the preservice teachers mean to the students at the school. This is followed by a parent and other staff members, who describe how they see service-learning fitting into the school culture and curriculum, recount some of their favorite experiences with service-learning, and explain the logistics of getting supplies, conducting fund-raising, and arranging field trips.

I usually take a few moments to summarize the requirements of the field experience for everyone, including key school personnel, allowing them to hear and ask questions. One of the most important speakers in the morning is one of the classroom teachers, who explains the wishes of the classroom teachers concerning preparing and cleaning up after projects, planning for field trips, contacting teachers at home, and giving clear directions to students. Sometimes we are able to have a guest speaker, such as a Department of Education consultant, who sees service-learning programs statewide and can reflect on their importance for state proficiencies.

At the conclusion of the morning's activities, selected students from intermediate grade level classes conduct walking tours of the school community. During these informal times, preservice teachers get a chance to see the community and ask questions of the students they might not ask in a more formal setting. Following a lunch break, students return to the school to meet their assigned teachers and students, complete some initial class observations, and learn what units are being studied and what projects are of interest to each class. Sometimes preservice teachers conduct brainstorming sessions with students, and sometimes they just observe while students explain what they have been studying.

At the end of the observation time, preservice teachers reassemble as a group and listen to a panel of elementary students present some of their past experiences and opinions about service-learning and working with preservice teachers (PSTs, they call them). It is during this time that my students catch a glimpse of the meaning of service-learning and how their work in schools touches the lives of children. Following this panel discussion, preservice teachers once again have the opportunity to question the principal, staff members, and me. By the end of the day, their comfort level and commitment to the field experience have usually been greatly enhanced.

In addition to the careful orientation of the preservice teacher to the school setting, it has been important for us to arrange a planning time between the classroom teacher and the preservice teacher during which they can take student ideas that have been discussed and plan lessons and experiences that will form the basis for the service-learning project. At S. Ellen Jones Elementary, grant monies have been used to provide substitute teachers for a two-hour planning block for each teacher/preservice teacher pair. This planning pays big dividends in terms of the smooth functioning of the school, the comfort level and enthusiasm of the preservice teachers, and my ability to provide coaching and supervision to my students. In instances in which schools have not had grant monies for planning or cases in which only a few teachers in the school were involved in the field experiences, students have arranged these planning times independently to fit the schedules of the teacher and themselves.

CELEBRATE, CELEBRATE, CELEBRATE

At the end of each project, preservice teachers at IUS are asked to demonstrate their service and learning in two ways: a service-learning fair on campus and a schoolwide program at the field site. Although there have been variations with both of these activities, each provides a way to communicate not only information but also meaning. At the school sites, celebrations have ranged from in-class sharing, to a few classes coming together, to a schoolwide program with colorful balloons, T-shirts, singing, demonstrations, displays, and speakers. At S. Ellen Jones, the celebrations have been schoolwide, exciting, and filled with that all important "aha" for the preservice teacher. Because preservice teachers work with individual classes, they sometimes miss how collective efforts from a number of projects can build a culture of caring within a school. Student comments at the end of the semester often sound like "you never told us it was like this" or "I didn't realize the kids cared so much."

On campus, I ask each preservice teacher to demonstrate what he or she has been doing at the field site by participating in a service-learning fair. This is held during a regular class session and includes inviting neighboring classes to visit the exhibits. Preservice teachers must prepare an exhibit and explain their projects in terms of both the service and the learning accomplished during the semester with their K-12 students. This creates an authentic assessment setting for my students and replaces the traditional midterm exam with an exhibition opportunity. It also serves as an opportunity for pre-methods students to anticipate the nature of activities within the methods courses.

IN-SERVICE TEACHERS FACE SPECIAL CHALLENGES

Classroom teachers wishing to gain experience with service-learning frequently elect the graduate workshop in service-learning at IUS. We first began offering the course in the fall of 1996 as a three-hour course and have since adjusted the credit to one semester hour. Classes are held during three intensive weekends with an extended space in the middle of the semester for students to plan and implement a beginning service-learning project with their classes. As with the undergraduate students, the first sessions are filled with information, background material, and dialogue. Teachers gain practice in generating projects from required curricula and then return to school to explore ideas with their students. I provide consultation for individual projects as the semester progresses, and teachers return at the end of the semester to share the results of their work.

Students in my graduate classes have come from a variety of levels and subject areas, including elementary teachers, special education teachers, vocational teachers, and teachers who operate special units in hospitals or other institutions. Sometimes they face challenges particular to their situation that may affect their ability to implement a project. For instance, one teacher operated a classroom in a mental health facility where students were mostly short-term patients. Scissors and sharp pencils were not allowed. In addition, she was not allowed to use photographs of the students. If she took the children outside, some of them became "runners" (i.e., they attempted to leave the grounds without permission). In this case, the teacher was very challenged to come up with projects that would help the students shift the focus from themselves to others. She did manage, despite all of the limitations, to develop a project in which students made artificial flower arrangements and presented them to other patients within the facility.

Some graduate students will face other obstacles within their school, such as lack of transportation for a needed field trip, insufficient funds for supplies, or just the perception that learning should occur within the four walls of the classroom. It is important to recognize when a graduate student faces these concerns and provide flexibility in course requirements, additional psychological support, and resources when possible. If service-learning is a new idea to the community and local administrators are not knowledgeable about the goals of service-learning, it may be helpful to visit the school site and seek opportunities for discussion and explanation.

More often than not, graduate students who elect the service-learning workshop have found creative ways to engage their students in service based on curricular goals. Comments on their evaluations lead me to believe they sometimes take on projects that prove quite ambitious, and yet they find that engaging in service-learning has been very rewarding. Their sharing in class is rich with stories of both success and failure. They learn from each other, and I learn from them. Much of what concerns them is similar to the concerns of preservice teachers—particularly the issues of time, resources, and administrative support.

THE CHALLENGES FOR TEACHER EDUCATORS

Service-learning as a strategy for teacher education has a lot of potential, and yet the reflective educator must also acknowledge a few challenges. Service-learning takes the teacher educator into the community and into real situations with preservice and in-service teachers. In the community are real people with real problems, issues of resources and fairness, and uncharted waters. Any of these factors can become a concern for safety, frustration, or public relations. Supporting several service-learning projects simultaneously can also be extremely labor intensive. This makes time management, administrative support, and resources concerns for faculty as well as preservice and in-service teachers.

The university reward system can also be a challenge for the teacher educator committed to service-learning. Service-learning lends itself to an integrated approach to teaching, research, and service. Indeed, it becomes very hard to separate these activities within the context of service-learning pedagogy. Promotion and tenure rules usually require a classification of one's activities into one of the three traditional categories. Deans and other faculty must understand and support the work of the teacher educator who takes a more hands-on approach to teacher education.

Despite the challenges mentioned, service-learning provides an opportunity for the teacher educator to become involved at a level that produces meaningful results for preservice teachers and promising growth for K-12 students. Willis Harman talked about two stonecutters who were engaged in a similar activity.[16] He states, "Asked what they were doing, one answered, 'I'm squaring up this block of stone.' The other replied, 'I'm building a cathedral.' The first may have been underemployed; the second was not. Clearly what counts is not so much what work a person does, but what he perceives he is doing it for."[17] Like the stone cutter building a cathedral, teacher educators do important and significant work. Service-learning allows us to prepare teachers who have the knowledge and skills to be efficient and effective educators, but, more importantly, it allows us the opportunity to develop the dispositions and habits of mind that could transform their understanding about the meaning and purpose of their work with children.

Notes

1. R. M. Caine and G. Caine, *Making Connections: Teaching and the Human Brain* (Alexandria, Va.: Association for Supervision and Curriculum Development, 1991).
2. Rahima C. Wade, "Developing Active Citizens: Community Service-learning in Social Studies Teacher Education," *The Social Studies* 86 (1995): 122-128.
3. Robert Bhaerman, Karen Cordell, and Barbera Gomez, *The Role of Service-Learning in Education Reform* (Needham Heights, Mass.: Simon and Schuster, 1998); Rahima C. Wade, "Service-learning in Preservice Teacher Education," in *Community Service-learning: A Guide to Including Service in the Public School Curriculum*, ed. Rahima C. Wade (Albany: State University of New York Press, 1997), 314-330.
4. Wade, "Developing Active Citizens," 1995.
5. C. Allam and B. Zerkin, "The Case for Integrating Service-Learning into Teacher Preparation Programs," *Generator* 13 (1993): 11-13; R. Sullivan, "The Role of Service-Learning in Restructuring Teacher Education," paper presented at the annual meeting of the Association of Teacher-Educators, New Orleans, 1991.
6. S. Root, "Service-learning in Teacher Education: A Third Rationale," *Michigan Journal of Community Service-Learning* 1 (1994): 94-97.
7. Allam and Zerkin, "The Case for Integrating Service-Learning," 1993; J. Toole, P. Toole, B. Gomez, and C. Allam, *Possible Links between Community Service and Teacher Preparation* (Washington, D.C.: Council of Chief of State Officers, 1992); Rahima C. Wade and J. Anderson, "Community Service-Learning: A Strategy for Preparing Human Service Oriented Teachers," *Teacher Education Quarterly* 23 (1996): 59-74.
8. National Council for the Social Studies, *Expectations of Excellence: Curriculum Standards for Social Studies*, Bulletin 89 (Washington, D.C.: Author, 1994).
9. Rahima C. Wade and K. M. O'Reilly, "Service-Learning in Preservice Teacher Education: Understanding Cooperating Teachers' Experiences," *National Society for Experiential Education Quarterly* 24 (Winter 1998): 7-11, 35; Rahima C. Wade, J. B. Anderson, C. B. Yarbrough, J. A. Erickson, and T. Kromer, "Novice Teachers' Experiences with Community Service-learning," *Teaching and Teacher Education* 15 (1999): 667-684.
10. Wade, "Developing Active Citizens," 1995: 123.
11. M. Boyle-Baise, "Community Service-Learning for Multicultural Education: An Exploratory Study with Preservice Teachers," *Equity & Excellence In Education* 31 (1998): 52–60.
12. J. Vadeboncoeur, J. Rahm, D. Aguilera, and M. D. LeCompte, "Building Democratic Character through Community Experiences in Teacher Education," *Education and Urban Society* 28 (1996): 189-207.
13. L. Boyle-Baise, "Community Service-Learning for Multicultural Education: An Exploratory Study with Pre-service Teachers" (Paper presented at the College and University Faculty Assembly of National Council for the Social Studies, Cincinnati, Ohio, November 1997); Boyle-Baise, "Community Service-Learning for Multicultural Education," 1998; D. Hones, "Preparing Teachers for Diversity: A Service-Learning Approach" (Paper presented at the annual meeting of the American Educational Research Association, Chicago, Illinois [ERIC Document Reproduction No. ED 406 381, 1997]); S. Seigel, "Community Service-Learning: A Component to Strengthen Multicultural Teacher Education" (Paper presented at the American Educational Research Association Annual Meeting, New Orleans, Louisiana, 1994); Christine E. Sleeter, "Reflections on My Use of Multicultural and Critical Pedagogy When Students Are White," in *Multicultural Education, Critical Pedagogy, and the Politics of Difference*, ed. Christine E. Sleeter and Peter McLaren (New York: SUNY Press, 1995); K. Tellez, P. S. Hlebowitsh, M. Cohen, and P. Norwood, "Social Service Field Experiences and Teacher Education," in *Developing Multicultural Teacher Education Curricula*, ed. Joseph M. Larkin and Christine E. Sleeter (Albany: State University of New York Press, 1995), 65-78.
14. Rahima C. Wade and D. B. Yarbrough, "Community Service-Learning in Student Teaching: Toward the Development of an Active Citizenry," *Michigan Journal of Community Service-learning* 4 (1997): 42-55.
15. Joan Rose, "OTUS: The Story of a School-University Partnership" (Ph.D. diss., Indiana University, Bloomington, 1994).
16. Willis Harman, cited in Caine and Caine, *Making Connections*, 1991.
17. *Ibid.*, 91.

CHAPTER 6

CHALLENGES TO EFFECTIVE PRACTICE*
Rahima C. Wade

Based on my work with public school service-learning programs and my observations of the service-learning movement nationwide, I believe that the lack of service-learning practice in social studies programs can be explained by challenges in two arenas: the culture of public schooling and the practice of service-learning itself. In this chapter, I explore the challenges in each of these realms and offer suggestions for improving service-learning activities to meet social studies goals and objectives.

Service-learning advocates, by and large, have not devoted much effort to assessing either service-learning in schools or the national service-learning movement as a whole. Although there are some legitimate reasons for neglecting that inquiry—such as the fear that opponents might use criticism to undermine the movement—critical reflection is essential to improvement. The ideas in this chapter are offered in the spirit expressed by Purpel in his statement, "The best criticism ought not to disarm and neutralize but instead should serve to rearm and energize."[1] I have divided the problems facing service-learning into two categories. First, I address the dissonance between service-learning and the norms and values of most public schools. Second, I discuss some difficulties within service-learning itself.

THE CULTURE OF PUBLIC SCHOOLING
Many aspects of the current structure of public schools in the United States pose significant challenges to the practice of service-learning. Perhaps most pervasive and potentially daunting is the way public schools mirror society in placing a high value on individual success over collective well-being. The norm in public school classrooms at all grade levels is individual work (e.g., seat work, homework, tests, essays). Frequently, communication and collaboration among students are discouraged. Elementary students, in particular, are often admonished to "keep your eyes, hands, and feet to yourself." High schools are typically characterized by fifty-minute, single-subject classes in which the teacher lectures the students and tests them individually on the material of the course.

The focus on individualism goes beyond the students to other aspects of school life. Schools do not generally encourage collaboration among teachers or between school and community. The public school structure makes collaboration difficult; most teachers do not have telephones in their classrooms, nor do they have many minutes in the school day to make or receive phone calls. Although some schools encourage shared planning time or team teaching, most often teachers are not provided with long lunch hours for meetings or discussion or with congruent planning periods.

---

* This chapter is taken from R. C. Wade, "Community Service-Learning and the Social Studies Curriculum: Challenges to Effective Practice" *The Social Studies* 88 (September/October 1997): 197-202. Reprinted by permission.

Teachers frequently mention another challenge as a major barrier to implementing service-learning in their classrooms, and that is time.[2] Teachers need considerable time to plan and coordinate site-specific activities, collaborate with others, think creatively about how to tie service to the curriculum, and make logistical arrangements for funding, transportation, and student supervision. Some teachers note that even if they had the time to do all of those tasks, they would still have difficulty finding time to fit service-learning projects into the school day, given all of the other demands in an increasingly overcrowded curriculum. Teachers who are not skilled in blending service with academics may view service-learning as valuable, but nonetheless a time-consuming "add-on."

Another challenge to service-learning in public schooling is the pervasive notion of "learning" as the memorization of factual information. Teachers who believe that their primary or only role is to present information to students and have them answer the questions in a textbook or take a test to determine how much of a lecture has been retained are unlikely to take the time and make the effort needed to implement service-learning activities in their classrooms. Research has shown that students learn by constructing meaning from their experience,[3] but schools seldom provide the direct experience and subsequent reflection that learning requires. The reflection component is a critical aspect of service-learning programs. Indeed, in a meta-analysis of research studies on community service and service-learning, Conrad and Hedin found that reflection was the single necessary element in a service program's leading to learning by students.[4] The notion that important information lies in students' experiences and the processing of those experiences, rather than only in external authorities or textbooks, is an alien idea in many school settings.

Service-learning projects focus on more than fact retention; they provide students with the opportunities to develop knowledge, skills, and attitudes that can be applied to real life situations. Community activities such as service-learning bring students in contact with a wide variety of people and tasks, and thus provide opportunities for personal and social development. Teachers who choose to include service in their curricula value those outcomes as well as their students' academic development.[5] Those who believe that the sole purpose of school is fact acquisition may think that service-learning is unnecessary, inappropriate, or a waste of time. The time issue may be critical, particularly for secondary social studies teachers faced with pressures to cover a specified amount of content in the textbook within a given period.

Schug and Beery have suggested several further difficulties for social studies teachers considering community activities in their curricula:

Community study requires more preparation by the teacher and student than other approaches to the social studies. Texts are not there to be evaluated, adopted, purchased, and used to give structure and substance to lessons. When there is so much that can be taught from textbooks and other standard curricular materials; when students resist being pushed out of the classroom to dig up, organize, and create their own information; when a variety of special interest groups become alarmed if young people probe real issues of the day, a harried social studies teacher might well ask: "Why bother?"[6]

These challenges can combine to produce an educational climate unsupportive of service-learning. If service-learning is to become a central part of public school social studies curricula, educators will need to respond with creativity and persistence to the challenges posed by the public school system. Three efforts may prove instrumental. First, when educators connect service-learning with compatible educational reform movements in their districts, they can often capitalize on prevailing funds, interest, and personnel. For example, some service-learning programs have been aligned with school-to work, drug education, dropout prevention, or authentic assessment initiatives.

Second, educators must make use of or develop suitable curriculum resources. See, for example, the Active Citizenship Today materials developed by the Constitutional Rights Foundation and the Close Up Foundation.[7] Those curriculum guides have been designed specifically for use in social studies classrooms. Other excellent curricular resources for service-learning programs are also available.[8] Many of the materials can be adapted for social studies programs.

In addition, many school districts are recognizing that they need to establish support systems for teachers involved with service-learning. Service-learning coordinators, teacher mentors, or peer consultants can assist in building a climate of collaboration in the school. School systems that expect teachers to engage in service-learning over the long term need to take the time problem seriously; many creative options exist for scheduling, staffing, and other supports that can make the difference for busy teachers. For example, in a midwestern university/public school service-learning program, teachers are provided with assistance from teacher-education students, use of service-learning resource "kits" on themes of interest (e.g., intergenerational, environmental), and paid planning time at school-site workshops. Teachers will always be challenged by the problem of available time, but supports such as these help many teachers continue to implement service-learning without "burning out."

Service-learning programs will have to fit within existing public school structures and, at the same time, attempt to transform them. Schools that have adopted a more student-centered, authentic approach to learning with flexible scheduling and collaborative teaching and learning structures will undoubtedly have an easier time adopting service-learning programs. More traditional schools will be challenged either to adapt service-learning practice to fit the school culture or to make structural changes in the school to support service-learning programs.

No matter what the type of school, the concept of such programs will spread if teacher educators, as part of their teacher preparation programs, train preservice teachers in the methods of service-learning. Through such involvement, preservice teachers can develop reflective thinking skills, become aware of community resources, and assist diverse students in learning through authentic instruction.[9] With the increase in many types of school and community collaborations, teachers trained in service-learning can be instrumental in bringing needed social services to students and their families.[10] Teacher educators have developed many approaches to infusing service-learning in the curriculum, from methods courses or practicum experiences to special courses in service-learning to projects completed during student teaching.[11]

THE PRACTICE OF SERVICE-LEARNING

Many problems beset the practice of service in school-based programs. First, too many service-learning projects focus on fund-raising, collections, or other indirect activities that may alleviate guilt but do little to build the solidarity and communal relationships characteristic of quality service-learning. Even when students interact with members of the community, service is often expressed as "do-gooding." Barber has contended that the focus of service-learning should be on citizenship, not charity.[12] Young people should focus not on helping "different" others with "their" problems but rather on "serving a public good that is also their own."[13] Sigmon has noted the lack of a sense of shared community in educators' comments about "using" the community and its agencies for students to gain experience, explore a career path, test a theory in practice, or do something for someone in need.[14]

That withdrawal from connection with others in the community is representative of the society's valuing of private over civic virtue. Brandhorst has noted that whereas there is evidence that young people are drawn to community service activities that involve caring about others and "feeling good" about oneself as a result, there appears to be little interest in public citizenship.[15] Newmann has asserted that a curriculum designed to prepare youth for future participation in one form does not necessarily prepare them for participation in another.[16] Thus, it is important that educators develop service-learning projects that support curricular goals and objectives. Social studies educators, in particular, should think carefully about how to structure service-learning projects that will enhance students' understanding of and commitment to being involved in the democratic process. The examples of service-learning projects in Chapters 2 through 4 of this bulletin illustrate just a few of the many ways social studies educators can frame service-learning within the context of civic action and public virtue. Students must be encouraged to look beyond their individual interests and seek the interest of the community at large. Furthermore, if social studies educators strive to develop their students' commitment to political action, they will probably be successful if they choose service activities dealing with government or political issues.

Without a concern for the future of society as a whole, students are less likely to consider the historical or societal contexts influencing the social issues that they may be addressing on a small scale with individuals or a single agency in their communities. Schultz has asserted that it is possible to become so intent on the problems at hand that students "lose awareness of the larger historical and contemporary forces acting on the present situation."[17] "This can lead to inappropriate action and an inability on the part of the student to generalize from present to subsequent action."[18] In too many service-learning programs, students simply accept the societal situations they confront "as they are," without questioning what might be needed for broad-based social change or developing an imaginative vision of how we could live together in more just and humane ways.[19]

Schneider has suggested that one of the ways that service-learning programs can become part of the solution rather than part of the problem is for the program leaders to ask significant and probing questions about the agencies where students are working and the underlying causes of the problems they are addressing.[20] Through such an approach, social studies teachers can incorporate the study of historical and societal issues into the service-learning project. Students must be taught to question the status quo, to examine stereotypes, to look beneath appearances in identifying causes, to seek out diverse opinions from varying information sources, and to be bold enough to envision more just and equitable ways of structuring our democratic society.

Service-learning projects in multicultural settings present a further challenge. The many barriers to equality that currently exist among people of different cultures in our society cannot be ignored in the design and conduct of service-learning programs. Purpel has noted that the potential exists for miscommunication, cultural misunderstanding, and even bewilderment in projects in which students from a dominant culture serve the marginalized members of society.[21] He has also asserted the possibility of the service fostering

> a sense of arrogance and condescension on the part of those who presume to know and act to intervene for what is best for other people . . . Lurking in the background of such relationships is the very real possibility of enhanced resentment, guilt, humiliation, and alienation for all involved which can culminate in the pain of embittered polarization.[22]

Cruz has posited that "in the context of conflicting interests and historical dominance of one racial or gender group over another, it is possible that 'service,' in and of itself, can have racist or sexist outcomes despite good intentions."[23] Thus, it is possible that although service-learning might empower the student, it might not promote the common good if it reinforces a sense of inferiority among those served or superiority among those who do the serving.[24] Historically, wealthy Americans have been in a position to bestow or withhold aid, whereas people receiving help are placed in a dependent position, needing to fit into the expectations of those giving aid and often in the role of always looking to others to provide very basic help.[25]

There are no easy answers to the question of how to structure service-learning experiences between individuals from different cultures or socioeconomic levels. Sigmon has advocated listening to those whose voices have traditionally been marginalized.[26] He has suggested that program leaders focus on expanding that limited relationship and "slow down, even curtail some of our direct service work, and examine what we are doing, by going into communities and organizations to 'sit down, be quiet, and pay attention.'"[27] Through that process, according to Sigmon, educators will "begin to hear of creative ways we can relate in mutual serving and learning across the boundaries of gender, race, age, credentials, economic status, national origin, faith, and educational attainment."[28]

Cruz has asserted that it might be best to focus on the learning that can be shared between people, rather than on "service," per se.[29] When possible, social studies teachers should seek projects in which the boundaries between server and served become blurred through mutual goal setting and collaboration. Although none of these ideas is a panacea for the problem of societal inequities, all may possess potential for service-learning practice that fosters more equitable relationships and empowers those involved.

Another equally challenging concern is the efficacy of service. Whether or not service activities actually have a long-term impact on social and environmental problems remains a question. Some educators have noted that service-learning activities, in and of themselves, are unlikely to change the deeply structured inequities in our society.[30] Purpel has pointed out that "relatively modest successes can actually exacerbate problems through the process of co-optation in which amelioration serves to prop up the very structures that created the problems in the first place."[31] Gorham has underscored that view and asserted the importance of advocacy activities in service-learning programs.[32] Recognizing the limitations of service-learning activities, Leeds has urged taking a realistic view about how much service projects can accomplish.[33] "Grandiosity is the enemy of a well-thought-out, inevitably small-scale attempt to make some impact on several overwhelming social problems. At its best, service will demonstrate not only how much students and others might do but how much more needs to be done and thought about."[34]

One reasonable response to this dilemma is to set realistic goals for what can be accomplished through service-learning projects. Service-learning practitioners need to imbue their work with a sense of reality and humility. Service-learning programs may not rid society of its ills, yet the limited gains they do accomplish can be heartening. "Problems surely can and should be ameliorated, suffering and pain reduced, justice and equity increased, peace furthered, violence lessened, meaning strengthened."[35] Furthermore, students can reflect on their service experiences, considering the underlying root causes for the problems they are addressing and develop ideas, as well as actual activities, for advocacy efforts aimed at altering larger structural concerns.

TOWARD A FUTURE FOR SERVICE-LEARNING

For service-learning to thrive in social studies programs in the future, many challenges must be met. Research studies focused on the outcomes of service-learning for students and communities must be generated to support the promising findings thus far and the substantial anecdotal evidence that supports the concept. In particular, studies are needed on effective service-learning practices that enhance social studies objectives. A study that involved interviewing social studies teachers about their decision of whether or not to be involved with service-learning would provide practical information for the field.

In addition to research studies, attention must be paid to the logistical aspects of service-learning. A need exists for more curriculum materials focused on social studies content and objectives. Funding for project materials, transportation, and personnel to help coordinate the many logistical aspects of conducting service-learning activities must be secured. Controversies about whether or not it is legitimate to require students to complete service activities outside the time frame of the school day must be resolved. In general, if educators believe in the learning value of service-learning, they should strive to include opportunities for service within school hours.

CONCLUSION

Although considerable work still needs to be done to infuse service-learning effectively into the social studies, the effort is well justified. Social studies educators must avoid programs that result in simple "feel good" exercises and embrace those that foster learning about and embracing the notion of public virtue. Community participation in a democratic society should not be simply an option: it is both a right and responsibility. It is the schools' obligation and social studies' mission to develop students who have the skills, knowledge, and attitudes to participate as informed and active members of their communities.

Despite the current shortcomings of service-learning practice in schools, educators should be encouraged by the potential that service-learning offers to reinvigorate the social studies curriculum and actualize the meaning of citizenship. Purpel concluded his critique of service-learning with the following affirmation:

> Humanity's greatest achievement would seem to be its persistence in its aspiration for goodness in the face of the incredible pressures for mere survival and self-enhancement. The arrival of the service-learning movement signals that this impulse has been re-energized with fresh urgency and hope.[36]

Notes

1. D. Purpel, "Service Learning: A Critique and Affirmation" (Paper presented at the annual meeting of the American Educational Research Association, San Francisco, California, April 18-22, 1995), 4.

2. Rahima C. Wade, "Contextual Influences on Teachers' Experiences with Community Service Learning" (Paper presented at the annual meeting of the American Educational Research Association, San Francisco, California, April 15-20, 1995a); Rahima C. Wade and W. M. Eland, "Connections, Rewards, and Challenges," *National Society for Experiential Education Quarterly* 21 (1995): 4-5, 26-27.

3. J. G. Brooks and M. Brooks, *In Search of Understanding: The Case for Constructivist Classrooms* (Alexandria, Va.: Association for Supervision and Curriculum, 1993); R. S. Prawat, "From Individual Differences to Learning Communities—Our Changing Focus," *Education Leadership* 47 (1992): 9-13.

4. D. Conrad and D. Hedin, *Executive Summary of the Final Report of the Experiential Education Evaluation Project* (Minneapolis: University of Minnesota Center for Youth Development and Research, 1982).

5. Wade, "Contextual Influences on Teachers' Experiences," 1995a.

6. Mark C. Schug and Robert Beery, *Community Study: Applications and Opportunities*, Bulletin 73 (Washington, D.C.: National Council for the Social Studies, 1984), 1.

7. See, for example, the Active Citizenship Today materials developed by Close Up Foundation and Constitutional Rights Foundation, *Active Citizenship Today* (Alexandria, Va.: Close Up Foundation, 1995).

8. Rich W. Cairn, with T. L. Coble, *Learning by Giving: K-8 Service-Learning Curriculum Guide* (St. Paul, Minn.: National Youth Leadership Council, 1993); Iowa Service-Learning Partnership, *Joining Hands Community Service-learning Resource Kits K-8* (Iowa City: Author, 1995; available from Service-Learning Department, Seashore Hall Center, University of Iowa, Iowa City, IA 52242); Maryland Student Service Alliance, "The Courage to Care, the Strength to Serve: Draft Instructional Framework in Service Learning" (Baltimore, Md.: Author, 1992); L. S. Stephens, *The Complete Guide to Learning through Community Service Grade K-9* (Boston: Allyn and Bacon, 1995).

9. C. Allam, "The Case for Integrating Service Learning into Teacher Preparation Programs," *The Generator* 13 (1993): 11-13; S. Root, "Service Learning in Teacher Education: A Third Rationale," *Michigan Journal of Community Service Learning* 1 (1994): 94-97.

10. Rahima C. Wade and J. Anderson, "Community Service-Learning: A Strategy for Preparing Human Service Oriented Teachers," *Teacher Education Quarterly* 23 (1996): 59-74.

11. Rahima C. Wade, "Developing Active Citizens: Community Service-Learning in Social Studies Teacher Education," *The Social Studies* 86 (1996): 122-128; Wade and Anderson, "Community Service-Learning."

12. Benjamin Barber, *An Aristocracy of Everyone: The Politics of Education and the Future of America* (New York: Ballantine, 1992).

13. *Ibid.*, 256.

14. R. L. Sigmon, "Sit Down. Be Quiet. Pay Attention." *National Society for Experiential Education Quarterly* 20 (1995): 31.

15. A. R. Brandhorst, "What Can Social Science Research Tell Us about Community Service and the Social Studies" (Paper presented at the annual meeting of National Council for the Social Studies, Anaheim, California, November 15 [ERIC Document Reproduction No. ED 338 512, 1990]).

16. Fred M. Newmann, "Reflective Civic Participation," *Social Education* 53 (1989): 357-366.

17. S. K. Schultz, "Whither Civic Education: Classics or Community Service?" The *Education Digest* 56 (1991): 56-60.

18. *Ibid.*, 59.

19. *Ibid.*

20. J. A. Schneider, "Fostering Equality through Service Learning," *National Society for Experiential Education Quarterly* 21 (1995): 10-11.

21. Purpel, "Service Learning," 1995.

22. *Ibid.*, 2.

23. N. Cruz, "A Challenge to the Notion of Service," in *Combining Service and Learning: A Resource Book for Community and Public Service*, Volume 1, ed. J. C. Kendall and associates (Raleigh, N.C.: National Society for Experiential Education, 1990), 322.

24. *Ibid.*

25. Schneider, "Fostering Equality," 1995.

26. Sigmon, "Sit Down," 1995.

27. *Ibid.*, 31.

28. *Ibid.*, 31.

29. Cruz, "A Challenge to the Notion of Service," 1990.
30. Eric Gorham, *National Service, Citizenship, and Political Education* (Albany: State University of New York Press, 1992); J. Leeds, "National Service: The Challenge," *National Society for Experiential Education Quarterly* 20 (1994): 16-17; Purpel, "Service Learning," 1995.
31. Purpel, "Service Learning," 1995: 3.
32. Gorham, *National Service*, 1992.
33. Leeds, "National Service," 1994.
34. *Ibid.*, 16.
35. Purpel, "Service Learning," 1995: 12.
36. *Ibid.*, 12.

RESOURCES FOR SOCIAL STUDIES EDUCATORS

CURRICULUM GUIDES

Active Citizenship Today Program. *ACT Field Guide (high school)*. Alexandria, VA: Close Up Foundation, 1994.

Active Citizenship Today Program. *ACT Field Guide (middle school)*. Alexandria, VA: Close Up Foundation, 1995.

Active Citizenship Today Program. *ACT Handbook for Teachers (high school)*. Alexandria, VA: Close Up Foundation, 1994.

Active Citizenship Today Program. *ACT Handbook for Teachers (middle school)*. Alexandria, VA: Close Up Foundation, 1995.

Adams, P., and J. Marzollo. *The Helping Hands Handbook*. New York: Random Books Young Readers, 1992.

American Bar Association's Special Committee on Youth Education for Citizenship. *Servicing the Community: Lawyers Helping Young People Become Good Citizens*. Chicago: American Bar Association, 1996.

Berry, J. *Every Kid's Guide to Saving the Earth*. Nashville, TN: Hambleton-Hill, 1993.

Cairn, R., and J. Kielsmeier. *Growing Hope: A Source Book on Integrating Youth Service into the School Curriculum*. Roseville, MN: National Youth Leadership Council, April 1991.

Cairn, R., and T. L. Coble. *Learning by Giving: K-8 Service-Learning Curriculum Guide*. Roseville, MN: National Youth Leadership Council, 1993.

Constitutional Rights Foundation. *Service Learning in the Social Studies*. Chicago: Constitutional Rights Foundation.

Dee, C., ed. *Kid Heroes of the Environment*. Berkeley, CA: Earth Works Press, Inc, 1991.

Fiffer, S., and S. S. Fiffer. *Fifty Ways to Help Your Community: A Handbook for Change*. New York: Main Street Books, 1994.

Goodman, A. *The Big Help Book; 365 Ways You Can Make A Difference By Volunteering*. New York: Pocket Books, 1994.

Hammond, M., and R. Collins. *One World One Earth: Educating Children for Social Responsibility*. Philadelphia, PA: New Society Publishers, 1993.

Hoose, P. *It's Our World, Too: Stories Of Young People Who Are Making A Difference*. Dubuque, IA: Little, Brown, 1993.

Isaac, K. *Civics for Democracy: A Journey for Teachers and Students.* Washington, DC: Center for Study of Responsive Law and Essential Information, 1989.

Kroloff, C. A. *Fifty-Four Ways You Can Help the Homeless.* Southport, CT & West Orange, NJ: Hugh Lauter Leven Assoc. Inc. & Behrman House, Inc., 1993.

Kronenwetter, M. *Taking a Stand Against Human Rights Abuses.* New York: Franklin Watts, 1990.

Lewis, B. A. *The Kid's Guide to Social Action: How to Solve the Social Problems You Choose and Turn Creative Thinking into Positive Action.* Minneapolis, MN: Free Spirit Publishing, Inc., 1991.

Lewis, B. A. *The Kids Guide to Service-Projects.* Minneapolis, MN: Free Spirit Publishing, Inc., 1995.

Lions-Quest International. *Skills for Growing.* Granville, OH: Quest International, 1990.

Logan, S. *The Kids Can Help Book.* New York: Perigree Books, 1992.

Maryland Student Service Alliance. *High School Service-Learning Guide.* Baltimore, MD: Maryland State Department of Education, 1993.

Maryland Student Service Alliance. *The Courage to Care, The Strength to Serve: Draft Instructional Framework in Service-Learning for Elementary Schools.* Baltimore, MD: Maryland State Department of Education, 1991b.

Maryland Student Service Alliance. *The Courage to Care, The Strength to Serve: Draft Instructional Framework in Service-Learning for Middle Schools.* Baltimore, MD: Maryland State Department of Education, 1991a.

McKissack, P., and F. McKissack. *Taking a Stand Against Racism and Racial Discrimination.* New York: Franklin Watts, 1990.

Meltzer, M. *Who Cares? Millions Do.* New York: Walker & Co, 1994.

National Youth Leadership Council. *Route to Reform: K-8 Service-Learning Curriculum Ideas.* St. Paul, MN: National Youth Leadership Council, 1994.

Newkirk, I. *Save the Animals: 101 Easy Things You Can Do.* New York: Warner Books, Inc., 1990.

Social Science Education Consortium. *Service Learning in the Middle School Curriculum: A Resource Book.* 1996.

Stephen, L. S. *The Complete Guide to Learning Through Community Service Grades K-9.* Des Moines, IA: Allyn & Bacon, 1995.

University of Iowa Service-Learning Department. *Joining Hands Community Service Learning Resource Kits.* University of Iowa: Author, 1997.

Wade, R., ed. *Community Service-Learning: A Guide to Including Service in the Public School Curriculum.* Albany, NY: State University of New York Press, 1997.

BOOKS AND JOURNAL ARTICLES

Allen, R. F. "Bibliographic Resources for School-Based Community Service Learning." *The Social Studies* 88, no. 5 (September/October 1997): 220-224.

Alliance for Service-Learning in Education Reform. *Standards of Quality for School-based Service-Learning.* Chester, VT: Alliance for Service-Learning in Education Reform, 1993.

Barber, B. "Public Talk and Civic Action: Education for Participation in a Strong Democracy." *Social Education* 53 (1989): 355-356, 370.

Bidlack, C., and R. Williams. "The Magic of Elsah Creek." *Social Education* 57, no. 6 (October 1993): 372-380.

Boyer, E. L. "Civic Education for Responsible Citizens" *Educational Leadership* 48 (1990): 4-7.

Boyte, H. C. "Community Service and Civic Education." *Phi Delta Kappan* 72 (June 1991): 765-767.

Brandell, Mary Ellen, and Shelly Hinck. "Service Learning: Connecting Citizenship with the Classroom." *NASSP Bulletin* 81, no. 591 (October 1997): 49-56.

Clark, T. "Youth Community Service." *Social Education* 53 (1989): 367.

Conrad, D., and D. Hedin. "School-Based Community Service: What We Know from Research and Theory." *Phi Delta Kappan* 72 (1991): 743-749.

Cumbo, Kathryn Blash, and Jennifer A. Vadeboncoeur. "What are Students Learning?: Assessing Cognitive Outcomes in K-12 Service-Learning." *Michigan Journal of Community Service Learning* 6 (Fall 1999): 84-96.

Fertman, C. *Service Learning for All Students: Fastback 375.* Bloomington, IN: Phi Delta Kappa Educational Foundation, 1994.

Fertman, C. I., White, G. P., and L. J. White. *Service Learning in the Middle School: Building a Culture of Service.* Columbus, OH: National Middle School Association, 1996.

Finger, William. "Service-Learning in the Community—Are We Ready for the Journey?" *National Society for Experiential Education Quarterly* 23, no. 3 (Spring 1998): 4-5, 23-25.

Garman, B. *Civic Education Through Service Learning.* ERIC-CHESS (EDO-SO-95-4).

Gavin, Connie, Libresco, Andrea, and Paula Marron. "Essential Questions for Elementary Social Studies: Curriculum Reform for Social Action." *Social Studies and the Young Learner* 11, no. 3 (January/February 1999): 12-15.

Gorham, E. B. *National Service, Citizenship, and Political Education.* Albany, NY: State University of New York Press, 1992.

Hamot, Greg E., with Marlene Johnson. "Enriching Economics through Global Education and Service Learning: Fifth Graders Rally Around the Rain Forest." *Social Studies and the Young Learner* 11, no. 2 (November/December 1998): 18-21.

Harwood, Angela M., and Jenel Chang. "Inquiry-Based Service Learning and the Internet." *Social Studies and the Young Learner* 12, no. 1 (September/October 1999): 15-18.

Harwood, Angela M., and Callie Underhill. *Promising Practice for K-16 Project Connect: School-University Collaboration for Service-Learning.* Denver, CO: Education Commission of the States, 2000.

Hess, Diana. "Violence Prevention and Service Learning." *Social Education* 61, no.5 (September 1997): 279-281.

Honnet, E. P., and S. J. Poulsen. *Principles of Good Practice for Combining Service and Learning.* Racine, WI: The Johnson Foundation, October 1989.

Kahne, J., and J. Westheimer. "In the Service of What? The Politics of Service Learning." *Phi Delta Kappan* 77, no. 9 (May 1996): 593-599.

Kaye, C. B. "Learning Through Caring: Students Serve Their Communities." *Teaching Tolerance* 2 (Spring 1993): 13.

Kinsley C. W., and K. McPherson, eds. *Enriching the Curriculum Through Service Learning.* Alexandria, VA: Association for Supervision and Curriculum Development, 1995.

Kirby, K. "Community Service and Civic Education." *ERIC Digest* (EDO-SO-89-8).

Lewis, B. A. "Cleanup Crusade: Citizenship in Action." *Social Education* 54 (1990): 238-240.

Lewis, B. A. "Serving Others Hooks Gifted Students on Learning." *Educational Leadership* 53, no. 5 (February 1996): 70-74.

The Make A Difference Day Planning Group. "Make a Difference: Elementary Service Projects." *Social Studies and the Young Learner* 12, no. 4 (March/April 2000): 14-16.

Miller, B, and L. R. Singleton. *Preparing Citizens: Linking Authentic Assessment and Instruction in Civic/Law-Related Education.* Boulder, CO: Social Science Education Consortium, 1997.

Mittlefehldt, W. "Proactive Citizenship and Service Learning at Anoka High School." *Social Studies* 88, no. 5 (September/October 1997): 203-209.

National Center for Service Learning in Early Adolescence. *Connections: Service Learning in the Middle Grades.* New York: National Center for Service Learning in Early Adolescence, 1991a.

National Center for Service Learning in Early Adolescence. *Reflection: The Key to Service Learning.* New York: National Center for Service Learning in Early Adolescence, 1991b.

Newmann, F. "Reflective Civic Participation." *Social Education* 53 (1989): 357-360.

Newmann, F., and R. Rutter. "A Profile of High School Community Service Programs." *Educational Leadership* 43 (1986): 65-71.

Oswald, J. M. "Resource Review: Serving to Learn, Learning to Serve–Civics and Service from A to Z by Cynthia Parsons." *Social Studies* 88, no. 5 (September/October 1997): 225-226.

Ottennitter, Nan, and C. David Lisman. "Weaving Service-Learning into the Fabric of Your College." *National Society for Experiential Education Quarterly* 23, no. 3 (Spring 1998): 10-11, 26-28.

Proctor, D. R., and M. E. Haas. "Social Studies and School-based Community Service Programs: Teaching the Role of Cooperation and Legitimate Power." *Social Education* 57, no. 7 (November/December 1993): 381-384.

Roebuck, D., and A. Hochman. "Community Service Agencies and Social Studies: A New Partnership." *Social Education* 57, no. 2 (February 1993): 76-77.

Shaheen, J. C. "Participatory Citizenship in the Elementary Grades." *Social Education* 53 (October 1989): 361-63.

Thompson, S. "The Community as Classroom." *Educational Leadership* 52 (May 1995): 17-20.

Totten, S., and J. E. Pedersen, eds. *Social Issues and Service at the Middle Level.* Needham Heights, MA: Allyn & Bacon, 1997.

The United Nations Global Teach-In Project and the American Forum for Global Education. "Schools Demining Schools: A Global Teach-In." *Social Education* 62, no. 5 (September 1998): 258-265.

Wade, R. "Beyond Charity: Service Learning for Social Justice." *Social Studies and the Young Learner* 12, no. 4 (March/April 2000): 6-9.

–––––. "Community Service-Learning: Commitment through Active Citizenship." *Social Studies and the Young Learner* 6 (January-February 1994): 1-4.

–––––. "Developing Active Citizens: Community Service Learning in Social Studies Teacher Education." *Social Studies* 86, 3 (May/June 1995): 122-128.

–––––. "Community Service Learning and the Social Studies Curriculum: Challenges to Effective Practice." *Social Studies* 88, no. 5 (September/October 1997): 197-202.

Wade, R., and D. W. Saxe. "Community Service-Learning in the Social Studies: Historical Roots, Empirical Evidence, and Critical Issues." *Theory and Research in Social Education* 24, no. 4 (Fall, 1996): 331-359.

Whitfield, Toni S. "Connecting Service- and Classroom-Based Learning: The Use of Problem-Based Learning." *Michigan Journal of Community Service Learning* 6 (Fall 1999): 106-111.

Willison, S. "When Students Volunteer to Feed the Hungry: Some Considerations for Educators." *Social Studies* 85 (March-April 1994): 88-90.

–––––. "Excerpts from Service Learning in the Social Studies." *Social Studies* 88, no. 5 (September/October 1997): 210-214.

—————. "Standards of Quality for School-Based and Community-Based Service Learning." *Social Studies* 88, no. 5 (September/October 1997): 215-219.

Wysocki, Barbara L. "Evaluating Students in a Course on Social Advocacy." *Social Education* 63, no. 6 (October 1999): 346-350.

NATIONAL ORGANIZATIONS

Alliance for Service Learning in Educational Reform
One Massachusetts Avenue NW, Suite 700
Washington, DC 20001
202-336-7026

Campus Compact
Brown University
Box 1975
Providence, RI 02912

Close Up Foundation
44 Canal Center Plaza
Alexandria, VA 22314-9836

Constitutional Rights Foundation
601 South Kingsley Drive
Los Angeles, CA 90005

Corporation For National and Community Service
1201 New York Avenue, NW
Washington, DC 20525

National Indian Youth Leadership Project
McClellan Hall
650 Vanderbosch Parkway
Gallup, NM 87301

National Service Learning Clearinghouse
University of Minnesota
Department of Work, Community and Family Education
1954 Buford Avenue, Room R-460
Saint Paul, MN 55108

National Society for Experiential Education
1703 N Beauregard Street, Suite 400
Raleigh, NC 27609

National Youth Leadership Council
1910 West County Road B
Saint Paul, MN 55113-1337

WORLD WIDE WEB RESOURCES

American Association for Higher Education Service-Learning Project
http://www.aahe.org/service/srv-lrn.htm

Compact for Learning and Citizenship Education Commission of the States
http://www.ecs.org

Campus Compact
http://www.compact.org

Close-Up Foundation
www.closeup.org

Constitutional Rights Foundation
http://www.crf-usa.org

Corporation for National Service
http://www.nationalservice.org

Corporation for National Service: Learn and Serve America
http://www.learnandserve.org

Learning in Deed: Making a Difference Through Service-Learning
An Initiative of the W.K. Kellogg Foundation
http://www.learningindeed.org

The Make a Difference Day Planning Group
http://www.usaweekend.com

Michigan Journal of Community Service Learning
http://www.umich.edu/~ocsl/mjcsl/

Michigan K-12 Service Learning Center
http://www.educ.msu.edu

National Peer-Based Service-Learning Training & Technical Assistance Exchange
http://www.lsaexchange.org

National Service-Learning Clearinghouse
http://www.nicsl.coled.umn.edu

National Society for Experiential Education
http://www.nsee.org

National Youth Leadership Council
http://www.nylc.org

Points of Light Foundation
http://www.pointsoflight.org

SERVICE-LEARNING: AN ESSENTIAL COMPONENT OF CITIZENSHIP EDUCATION

A Position Statement of National Council for the Social Studies
Prepared by the NCSS Citizenship Select Subcommittee
Approved by the NCSS Board of Directors, May 2000

RATIONALE

The mission of the social studies profession, since its inception, has been to develop informed and active citizens. To become responsible citizens, students must have access not only to content knowledge and core democratic values, but also to opportunities to learn citizenship skills and apply them to problems and needs in the community beyond the classroom. Service-learning provides essential opportunities for students not only to develop civic participation skills, values, and attitudes, but also to acquire first-hand knowledge of the topics they are studying in the curriculum. Service-learning provides an authentic means for using social studies content and skills to investigate social, political, and economic issues and to take direct action in an effort to create a more just and equitable society. Quality service-learning experiences may positively influence the following aspects of student development:

- Academic, problem solving, and critical thinking skills
- Ethical development and moral reasoning ability
- Social and civic responsibility
- Self-esteem, assertiveness, and empathy
- Political efficacy
- Tolerance and acceptance of diversity
- Career exploration

DEFINITION

Service-learning connects meaningful service in the school or community with academic learning and civic responsibility. Service-learning is distinguished from community service or volunteerism in two ways. First, the service activity is integrated with academic skills and content. Second, students engage in structured reflection activities on their service experiences. Quality service-learning activities meet a number of important criteria. In particular, they should:

- Provide opportunities for student and community input in the design of the service-learning experience;

- Engage students in both meaningful service and essential social studies content;
- Provide opportunities for reflection on the service experience and the connections between this experience, democratic values, and citizenship;
- Focus on change rather than charity, enabling students to question prevailing norms and develop new ideas for creating a more just and equitable society.

Effective service-learning projects go beyond simply using the community as a learning laboratory for student development. Of equal importance is the attempt to solve community problems, meet human and environmental needs, and advocate for changes in policies and laws to promote the common good. Through addressing real-life problems in their communities, students are challenged to work together to exercise the rights and responsibilities of democratic citizenship.

BENEFITS FOR SOCIAL STUDIES TEACHING AND LEARNING

Service-learning provides multiple benefits for social studies students, teachers, and their communities. First, service-learning activities provide relevant and motivational opportunities for students to connect the principles and processes of democratic life with practical community problem solving. Service-learning allows students to practice in the community the civic values and concepts they are learning in their social studies classrooms. With guided practice in collaborative problem solving, they learn that they can make a difference. In addition, the practical application of social science knowledge to community problems gives some students a much-needed stimulus to enhance their academic achievement.

Second, service-learning increases students' awareness of the community and world around them, the unmet needs in our society, the agencies and institutions involved in attempting to meet those needs, and a variety of strategies that they can use to create a better world. Through service-learning, students connect with real individuals and institutions working against injustice. They learn firsthand about the advantages of working as a group, the influence of public policy on human lives, and the intricacies of local government and community politics.

Finally, service-learning enhances the development of democratic values and attitudes. Not only do students develop firsthand knowledge of such abstract concepts as justice, diversity, opportunity, equality, and the common good, but they also develop empathy and compassion for others. Through direct experiences working with others in the community, students learn that American society is "unfinished," and that they can play a key role in narrowing the disparity between our democratic ideals and the reality of daily life.

CONCLUSION

National Council for the Social Studies believes that service-learning should be viewed as an essential component of social studies education in the 21st century. Service-learning greatly enhances the potential for social studies teachers to fulfill their mission of educating informed and active citizens who are committed to improving society through the democratic process. Students are less likely to become such citizens in a text-bound social studies curriculum that does not give them opportunities to practice their democratic rights and responsibilities and to contribute to the common good. For these reasons, NCSS strongly supports the integration of quality service-learning activities into the K-12 social studies curriculum as well as all social studies teacher education programs.

INDEX

A

B

C

I

J

K

L

M

BREATHE OUT FOR 4, HOLD FOR 4

(repeat 4 times)

CONCLUSION

My Cupboard of No Return has become a problem because I've left it so long it's now overwhelming. The only way I'm ever going to deal with it is by not viewing it as one huge job to tackle but realizing that I can break it down into a series of tiny actions. I need to put the left-hand glove with its right-hand partner, lock the passport in my filing cabinet and drop the golf ball into my Tupperware box in the shed. Easy! Before I know it, those shelves will be empty.

The stress in your life is no different to this. Now that you've read this book, I hope you've expanded your view of what stress is and have come to realize that it's lurking in many hidden places. MSDs are coming at you from all directions, pretty much all the time. There's nothing I can do about that. But what I can do is make you more resilient to them.

Without question, the L.I.V.E. framework is the most important intervention in this book. A life devoid of meaning and purpose will stress you out faster than anything else. I urge you to begin introducing this idea into your life today. When you do, you'll find it makes the other recommendations much easier to achieve. Remember, you don't need to do every single one. Don't look for perfection but for a balance across all four pillars.

You have in your hands a toolkit full of powerful interventions, most of which are both simple and free. If you enact enough of them, they'll turn you into a stress superhero, fighting off those MSDs as if you're surrounded by a forcefield of calm.

But you have to start small. Not every page of *The Stress Solution* is going to be relevant to your life. But I'd like you to pick an intervention which, when you saw it, truly resonated with you. One that truly struck a chord deep within and that made you think, 'I could do that right now.' It may well have been something easy – holding hands with your partner, breathing purposefully for sixty seconds, lighting some candles. That doesn't matter. Your world is defined not by the books you've read but by your actions. That simple intervention is your first step.

Take it.

REFERENCES

Introduction

Aditi Neurkar et al., 'When Physicians Counsel about Stress: Results of a National Study', 14 January 2013, https://jamanetwork.com/journals/jamainternalmedicine/fullarticle/1392494

PURPOSE

R. Cohen, C. Bavishi and A. Rozanski, 'Purpose in Life and Its Relationship to All-Cause Mortality and Cardiovascular Events: A Meta-analysis', February–March 2016, https://www.ncbi.nlm.nih.gov/pubmed/26630073

Andrew Steptoe, Angus Deaton and Arthur Stone, 'Subjective Wellbeing, Health and Ageing', 5 November 2014, https://www.thelancet.com/journals/lancet/article/PIIS0140-6736(13)61489-0/fulltext

Pia Hedberg et al., 'Depression in Relation to Purpose in Life among a Very Old Population: A Five-Year Follow-up Study', August 2010, https://www.ncbi.nlm.nih.gov/pubmed/20686985

Arlene D. Turner et al., 'Is Purpose in Life Associated with Less Sleep Disturbance in Older Adults?', 10 July 2017, https://sleep.biomedcentral.com/articles/10.1186/s41606-017-0015-6

The 3 Habits of Calm

Michael D. Wood et al., 'Buffering Effects of Benefit Finding in a War Environment', 4 March 2011, https://www.tandfonline.com/doi/abs/10.1080/08995605.2010.521732

J. David Cresswell et al., 'Affirmations Improve Student Performance in Undergraduates', 1 May 2013, http://journals.plos.org/plosone/article?id=10.1371/journal.pone.0062593

Jeremy P. Jamieson, Matthew K. Nock and Wendy Berry Mendes, 'Reappraising Stress Reduces Heart Rate', 26 September 2011, https://www.ncbi.nlm.nih.gov/pmc/articles/ PMC3410434/

Xianglong Zeng et al., 'Meta-analysis of Loving Kindness Meditation', 3 November 2015, https://www.ncbi.nlm.nih.gov/pmc/articles/PMC4630307/

Schedule Your Time

Grant Hilary Brenner, 'Your Brain and Creativity', 22 February 2018, https://www.psychology today.com/gb/blog/experimentations/201802/your-brain-creativity

RELATIONSHIPS

Human Touch

C. D. Walker, 'Maternal Touch and Feed as Critical Regulators of Behavioural and Stress Responses in the Offspring', November 2010, https://www.ncbi.nlm.nih.gov/pubmed /20862707

M. W. Kraus, C. Huang and D. Keltner, 'Tactile Communication, Co-operation and Performance: An Ethological Study of the NBA', October 2010, https://www.ncbi.nlm.nih. gov/pubmed/21038960

Mariana von Mohr, Louise P. Kirsh and Aikaterini Fotopolou, 'The Soothing Function of Touch: Affective Touch Reduces Feelings of Social Exclusion', 18 October 2017, https:// www.nature.com/articles/s41598-017-13355-7

F. McGlone, J. Wessberg and H. Olausson, 'Discriminative and Affective Touch: Sending and Feeling', 21 May 2014, https://www.ncbi.nlm.nih.gov/pubmed/24853935

J. A. Leonard et al., 'The Effect of Friendly Touch on the Delay of Gratification on Preschool Children', 2014, https://www.ncbi.nlm.nih.gov/m/pubmed/24666195/

Get Intimate

J. M. Twenge, R. A. Sherman and B. E. Wells, 'Declines in Sexual Frequency among American Adults, 1989–2014', 6 March 2014, https://www.ncbi.nlm.nih.gov/pubmed/28265779

Lancet, 'The Third National Survey of Sexual Attitudes and Lifestyles', 30 November 2013, https://www.thelancet.com/journals/lancet/issue/vol382no9907/PIIS0140-6736(13)X6059-3?code=lancet-site

J. A. Coan, H. S. Schaefer and R. J. Davidson, 'Lending a Hand: Social Regulation of the Neural Response to Threat', https://www.ncbi.nlm.nih.gov/pubmed/17201784

J. D. Meeker, A. M. Calafat and R. Houser, 'Urinary Bisphonol A Concentrations in Relation to Serum Thyroid and Reproductive Hormone Levels in Men from a Fertility Clinic', 15 February 2010, https://www.ncbi.nlm.nih.gov/pubmed/20030380

J. H. Mendelson, N. K. Mello and J. Ellingboe, 'Effects of Acute Alcohol Intake on Pituitary-Gonadal Hormones in Normal Human Males', September 1977, https://www.ncbi.nlm.nih.gov/pubmed/894528

Nurture Your Friendships

Mental Health Foundation, 'The Lonely Society?', 2 May 2010, https://www.mentalhealth.org.uk/sites/default/files/the_lonely_society_report.pdf

L. F. Berkman and S. L. Syme, 'Social Networks, Host Resistance, and Mortality: A Nine-Year Follow-up Study of Alameda County Residents', February 1979, https://www.ncbi.nlm.nih.gov/pubmed/425958

Nicole K. Valtorta et al., 'Loneliness and Social Isolation as Risk Factors for Coronary Heart Disease and Stroke: Systematic Review and Meta-analysis of Longitudinal Observational Studies', April 2016, https://heart.bmj.com/content/102/13/1009

George M. Slavich et al., 'Neural Sensitivity to Social Rejection Is Associated with Inflammatory Responses to Social Stress', 2 August 2010, https://www.ncbi.nlm.nih.gov/pmc/articles/PMC2930449/

BODY

Eat Yourself Happy

Lancet editorial, March 2015, https://www.thelancet.com/journals/lanpsy/article/ PIIS2215-0366%2814%2900051-0/abstract?code=lancet-site

R. F. Slykerman et al., 'Effect of *Lactobacillus rhamnosus* HN001 in Pregnancy on Postpartum Symptoms of Depression and Anxiety: A Randomised Double-Blind Placebo-Controlled Trial', October 2017, https://www.ncbi.nlm.nih.gov/pubmed/28943228

A. P. Allen et al., '*Bifidobacterium longum* 1714 as a Translational Psychobiotic: Modulation of Stress, Physiology and Neurocognition in Healthy Volunteers', 1 November 2016, https://www.ncbi.nlm.nih.gov/pmc/articles/PMC5314114/

Make Exercise Work For You

Timothy J. Shoenfeld et al., 'Physical Exercise Prevents Stress-Induced Activation of Granule Neurons and Enhances Local Inhibitory Mechanisms in the Dentate Gyrus', 1 May 2013, http://www.jneurosci.org/content/33/18/7770

Eli Puterman et al., 'The Power of Exercise: Buffering the Effect of Chronic Stress on Telomere Length', 26 May 2010, https://www.ncbi.nlm.nih.gov/pmc/articles/PMC2877102/

C. W. Janssen et al., 'Whole-Body Hyperthermia for the Treatment of Major Depressive Disorder: A Randomized Clinical Trial', 1 August 2016, https://www.ncbi.nlm.nih.gov/ pubmed/27172277

Reset Your Rhythm

Carla S. Möller-Levet et al., 'Effects of Insufficient Sleep on Circadian Rhythmicity and Expression Amplitude of the Human Blood Transcriptome', 25 February 2013, https:// www.ncbi.nlm.nih.gov/pmc/articles/PMC3607048/

Seung-Schik Yoo et al., 'The Human Emotional Brain without Sleep – a Prefrontal Amygdala Disconnect', 23 October 2017, https://www.cell.com/current-biology/fulltext/S0960-9822(07)01783-6?_returnURL=https%3A%2F%2Flinkinghub.elsevier.com%2Fretrieve%2Fpii%2FS0960982207017836%3Fshowall%3Dtrue

Anne Germain and Michael Dretsch, 'Sleep and Resilience – A Call for Prevention and Intervention', 1 May 2016, https://www.ncbi.nlm.nih.gov/pmc/articles/PMC4835317/

Tetsuya Matsubayashi, Yasayuki Sawada and Michio Ueda, 'Does the Installation of Blue Lights on Train Platforms Prevent Suicide? A Before-and-After Observational Study from Japan', May 2013, https://www.jad-journal.com/article/S0165-0327(12)00587-3/abstract

Amandine Chaix, 'Time-Restricted Feeding is a Preventative and Therapeutic Intervention against Diverse Nutritional Challenges', 2 December 2014, https://www.ncbi.nlm.nih.gov/pmc/articles/PMC4255155/

MIND

Technology Overload

Holly B. Shakya and Nicholas A. Christakis, 'Association of Facebook Use with Compromised Well-being: A Longitudinal Study', 1 February 2017, https://academic.oup.com/aje/article/185/3/203/2915143

Royal Society for Public Health Report, '#Status of Mind: Social Media and Young People's Health and Well-being' (n.d.), https://www.rsph.org.uk/our-work/campaigns/status-of-mind.html

Eric J. Vanman, Rosemary Baker and Stephanie J. Tobin, 'The Burden of Online Friends: The Effects of Giving Up Facebook on Stress and Well-being', 9 April 2018, https://www.tandfonline.com/doi/full/10.1080/00224545.2018.1453467

Adrian F. Ward et al., 'Brain Drain: The Mere Presence of One's Own Smartphone Reduces Available Cognitive Capacity', 3 April 2017, https://www.journals.uchicago.edu/doi/abs/10.1086/691462

Bathe Yourself in Nature

A. J. Park et al., 'The Physiological Effects of Shinrin-yoku (Taking in the Forest Atmosphere or Forest Bathing): Evidence from Field Experiments in 24 Forests across Japan', January 2010, https://www.ncbi.nlm.nih.gov/pubmed/19568835

Richard Taylor, 'Fractals in Psychology and Art', 3 February 2016, https://blogs.uoregon.edu/richardtaylor/2016/02/03/human-physiological-responses-to-fractals-in-nature-and-art/?xid=PS_smithsonian

Daniel K. Brown, Jo L. Barton and Valerie F. Gladwell, 'Viewing Nature Scenes Positively Affects Recovery of Autonomic Function Following Acute-Mental Stress', 6 April 2013, https://pubs.acs.org/doi/10.1021/es305019p

Take Time to Breathe

Kevin Yackle et al., 'Breathing Control Center Neurons that Promote Arousal in Mice', 31 March 2017, http://science.sciencemag.org/content/355/6332/1411

Xiao Ma et al., 'The Effect of Diaphragmatic Breathing on Attention, Negative Affect and Stress in Healthy Adults', 6 June 2017, https://www.ncbi.nlm.nih.gov/pmc/articles/PMC5455070/

Anup Sharma et al., 'A Breathing-Based Meditation Intervention for Patients with Major Depressive Disorder Following Inadequate Response to Antidepressants: A Randomized Pilot Study', January 2017, https://www.ncbi.nlm.nih.gov/pmc/articles/PMC5272872/

R. J. Davidson et al., 'Alterations in Brain and Immune Function Produced by Mindfulness Meditation', https://www.ncbi.nlm.nih.gov/pubmed/12883106

F. Kurth et al., 'Brain Gray Matter Changes Associated with Mindfulness Meditation in Older Adults: An Exploratory Pilot Study Using Voxel-Based Morphometry', https://www.ncbi.nlm.nih.gov/pubmed/25632405

M. K. Leung, 'Meditation-Induced Neuroplastic Changes in Amygdala Activity during Negative Affective Processing', https://www.ncbi.nlm.nih.gov/pubmed/28393652

ACKNOWLEDGEMENTS

To have completed my second book just twelve months after my first would simply not have been possible without the help and support of many people.

Vidhaata, for helping me understand who I really am.

Jainam and Anoushka, for ensuring that I never take my work too seriously and for reminding me on a daily basis of how to take pleasure in the small things in life. You drive me to improve myself and teach me how to become a better man. Both of you are special gifts and I love you more than words can say.

Mum, for showing me what unconditional love is. Your drive to keep pushing yourself and trying new things inspires me.

Dada, for always being there for me.

Jeremy, Ayan and Luke, for the many 'jam sessions' of new ideas over the phone, endlessly listening, giving feedback and, of course, for the friendship.

Mike, for the continued support, advice and mentorship.

Antony, for trusting your intuition.

Chetana and Dinesh, for teaching me how to look at life through a different lens. You have, without realizing it, helped shape many of the ideas in this book.

Dhru, for your amazing ability to bring the best out of people. I have been a grateful recipient on multiple occasions. You have influenced this book in many ways.

Steve and Carron, for being two of the finest friends I could ever have hoped to have.

Christian Platt, for your refreshing honesty, intuition and for opening my eyes to what is possible.

James and Dallas, for the brotherhood from across the pond.

Will Francis, you are simply the very best literary agent. This is just the start.

Clare Moore, for your ongoing dedication, willingness to take on new things and ability to cope with everything that is thrown at you.

Special thanks to Will Storr, Matthew Walker, Satchin Panda, Francis McGlone, Miguel Mateas, Alessandro Ferretti, Jodie Hawkey, Bobby Chatterjee, Ashley Tarran-Jones, Kelly Brogan, Gary Ward, Jo Murphy, Sophie, Carina and the whole team at Factual.

Nirav, Antonio and the whole team at Anatta – thanks for your advice, professionalism and for pushing me out of my comfort zone.

John and Susan, for your unmatched ability to bring my ideas to life with fresh ideas and your creative brilliance. Your input helps me reach many more people – thank you.

Venetia, Emily, Julia, Josie, Emma, Sarah and the rest of the team at Penguin Life – it is such a joy to be working alongside you all. Thanks for believing in me and the tireless support.

And finally, to each and every single one of my patients. You have taught me so much more than I have had the pleasure of teaching you.

INDEX

PURPOSE

NOTES

_____

_____

_____

_____

_____

_____

_____

_____

BODY

NOTES

_____

_____

_____

_____

_____

_____

_____

_____